9/2/10

Kelly—
Here's to your
new life of
independence and
city living.
Eat and
live well!
—Lynne

Good Housekeeping

FAST WEEKNIGHT FAVORITES

FAST WEEKNIGHT FAVORITES

200 Really Quick, Simply Delicious Recipes

HEARST BOOKS

A division of Sterling Publishing Co., Inc.

New York / London

www.sterlingpublishing.com

Good Housekeeping

Rosemary Ellis	Editor in Chief
Richard Eisenberg	Special Projects Director
Susan Westmoreland	Food Director
Susan Deborah Goldsmith	Associate Food Director
Delia Hammock	Nutrition Director
Sharon Franke	Food Appliances Director

Book design by Carolyn Veth Krienke
Book layout by Sandy Freeman

Library of Congress Cataloging-in-Publication Data
Good housekeeping : fast weeknight favorites : 200 really quick, simply delicious recipes / the editors of Good housekeeping magazine.
    p. cm.
  Includes index.
  ISBN 978-1-58816-719-4
 1. Entrées (Cookery) 2. Quick and easy cookery. I. Good Housekeeping magazine.
  TX740.G554 2008
  641.5'55--dc22

                                                                      2008011537

10 9 8 7 6 5 4 3 2 1

The Good Housekeeping Cookbook Seal guarantees that the recipes in this cookbook meet the strict standards of the Good Housekeeping Research Institute, a source of reliable information and a consumer advocate since 1900. Every recipe has been triple-tested for ease, reliability, and great taste.

Published by Hearst Books
A division of Sterling Publishing Co., Inc.
387 Park Avenue South, New York, NY 10016

Good Housekeeping and Hearst Books are trademarks of Hearst Communications, Inc.

www.goodhousekeeping.com

For information about custom editions, special sales, premium and corporate purchases, please contact Sterling Special Sales Department at 800-805-5489 or specialsales@sterlingpublishing.com.

Distributed in Canada by Sterling Publishing
c/o Canadian Manda Group, 165 Dufferin Street
Toronto, Ontario, Canada M6K 3H6

Distributed in Australia by Capricorn Link (Australia) Pty. Ltd.
P.O. Box 704, Windsor, NSW 2756 Australia

Manufactured in China

Sterling ISBN 978-1-58816-719-4

The Good Housekeeping Triple-Test Promise

At *Good Housekeeping*, we want to make sure that every recipe we print works in any oven, with any brand of ingredient, no matter what. That's why, in our test kitchens at the **Good Housekeeping Research Institute**, we go all out: We test each recipe at least three times—and, often, several more times after that.

When a recipe is first developed, one member of our team prepares the dish and we judge it on these criteria: it must be **delicious, family-friendly, healthy, and easy to make.**

1. The recipe is then tested several more times to fine-tune the flavor and ease of preparation, always by the same team member, using the same equipment.

2. Next, another team member follows the recipe as written, **varying the brands of ingredients** and **kinds of equipment.** Even the types of stoves we use are changed.

3. A third team member repeats the whole process **using yet another set of equipment** and **alternative ingredients.**

By the time the recipes appear on these pages, they are guaranteed to work in any kitchen, including yours. WE PROMISE.

Contents

Foreword

Like you, we in the Good Housekeeping food department juggle work, family, volunteer activities, and a social calendar. And like you, we often wonder what to put on the table at the end of the day to feed our families. *Fast Weeknight Favorites* is our solution to that dilemma. A day full of activities doesn't have to mean serving your family take-out food or frantic fussing in the kitchen to get dinner on the table. With *Fast Weeknight Favorites* as your kitchen companion and its tried-and-true recipes and time-saving tips, you can have a healthy, home-cooked meal ready in thirty minutes or less.

We've compiled these 200 fast and easy recipes to give you plenty of hassle-free entrées from which to choose. There are hearty dishes made with meat, fish, shellfish, poultry, and pasta, as well as tasty vegetarian selections. To help speed you on your way, many make use of convenience foods and pantry staples; and each employs one of several quick-cooking techniques, such as grilling, broiling, stir-frying, sautéing, and microwaving. You'll also find our most popular slow-cooker recipes.

The proof of any dish is in the tasting, of course. That's why we're so proud of our triple-test recipe policy (see page 6). So try our sweet-spicy Mongolian Beef Stir-fry, quick skillet Plum Balsamic Chicken, fifteen-minute Shrimp Scampi, or Sesame Salmon with Bok Choy. Whether you have vegetarians in your house or just like to serve an occasional meatless meal, check out spicy Nacho Casserole, elegant, rich Fusilli with Blue Cheese and Toasted Walnuts, ginger-and-curry-accented Vegetarian Lentil Stew, or one of our vegetarian pizzas, like Broccoli-Cheese Polenta Pizza.

We hope these and all the other dishes in *Fast Weeknight Favorites* will get raves from your family, and you'll enjoy being able to serve delicious, nourishing meals in under a half hour. But the express cooking is only one facet of *Fast Weeknight Favorites*. Planning, shopping, and organizing efficiently are the others. And who does these things better than you? So be sure to read the introduction for lots of great GH advice on ways to save time even before you begin to cook.

Take a break, sit down, and open *Fast Weeknight Favorites*. Select a recipe for tonight and we'll help you turn mealtime from a harried time in the kitchen into a relaxed dinner with your family.

Introduction

SERVE DELICIOUS WEEKNIGHT SUPPERS—FAST

It's the end of a busy day, you're running late, and there are still tons of things to do before you head home to start dinner. How you are ever going to put supper on the table? Trust us, preparing meals for your family that are quick, healthy, and delicious are not mutually exclusive goals. *Fast Weeknight Favorites* has 200 mouthwatering recipes for homemade dinners that are prepped and cooked in thirty minutes or less with ease—without sacrificing quality time with your family.

PLAN AHEAD

Keep it simple. Choose dishes with a limited number of ingredients that use simple cooking techniques. The aim is to spend dinnertime with your family, not to be bustling in the kitchen.

Make a list. Put aside some time once a week to plan menu ideas for the week ahead. Read recipes beforehand to be sure you have all the ingredients, either on hand or on your shopping list. Check your pantry for the staples you'll need or should replenish and your freezer and refrigerator for the necessary ingredients. Then plan your shopping list and keep it updated by adding any other items as you think of them.

Shop and stock. With shopping list in hand, navigate the supermarket for staples, sale items, and all the components you'll need for the week's menus. Doing a "big shopping" once a week and limiting or eliminating mid-week trips to the market is a simple yet effective time and money saver. Once you get home, be sure to wrap, pack, and store perishables properly.

Cook ahead. Weekends are great for making large batches of soups, stews, or casseroles. Serve some that evening and freeze the rest for another day. If you can, prepare a few basic foods that can be incorporated into meals during the week ahead: cook up a pot of rice or other grain, make pasta sauce, or roast some potatoes or a mix of seasonal vegetables.

SHOP SMART, SHOP QUICKLY

Most supermarkets are arranged in a similar manner: produce is in the front of the store; meats, dairy, deli, baked goods, and frozen items are usually found around the perimeter while the aisles are stocked with bottled, canned, and packaged goods. Arrange your shopping list by grocery departments and use it as a map to your local market. You'll know exactly where to find everything you need and won't waste time browsing. Start with the staples aisles first, move on to the perishables, then the refrigerated items. Save the frozen foods for last so they'll stay cold and cool the latter two.

Prepped and Premade Foods
Supermarkets carry a vast selection of foods that are available already prepared or prepped and make feeding a hungry family on the go a breeze.

- Prepared rotisserie chicken, chili, soups, pasta dishes, pot pies, etc., as well as salad bar items, can form the basis of a hearty no-cook dinner.
- Cleaned and cut, sliced, diced, shredded, and ready to use fresh vegetables can be found in the produce section along with packaged peeled and sliced fresh fruits.
- Packaged salad greens come cut, washed, and mixed with other veggies to go straight from the bag to the salad bowl.
- Frozen vegetables aren't just for side dishes. Available in a variety of styles and combinations, including ethnic mixes like Asian and Mediterranean, use them in a stir-fry or toss with noodles or pasta.
- Meats, fish, and poultry are sold in cuts from roasts to prepared kabobs, seasoned or marinated, and ready for grilling, steaming, stir-frying, and sautéing.
- Precooked and packaged chicken pieces, meatballs, and flavored sausages, for example, can help you get meals on the table in a flash.

Shopping Shortcuts
- Stock up when there's a sale on meats, poultry, seafood, or frozen foods you use. For meats, poultry, and seafood, separate what you plan to cook within two days and freeze the rest immediately. For quicker defrosting, wrap the items in meal-size portions.
- Choose items that naturally cook up fast: Use chicken tenders instead of whole chicken pieces; substitute thinly sliced medallions of pork instead of thick loin chops; select vegetables cut into the same matchstick-size pieces, which will cook evenly and more quickly than whole or large pieces.
- Take advantage of convenience products that are nutritious and have the fewest preservatives and artificial ingredients. Some of these include pre- or partially baked pizza shells, tortilla wraps, cooked deli meats, sliced cheeses, and prepared salads, such as coleslaw, broccoli slaw, carrot-and-raisin salad, potato salad, or spinach salad.
- Think outside the box—or bottle or package. *Flavored spice blends* in any of a variety of flavors can be mixed into ground beef for meatballs, burgers, or meatloaf with an exotic twist. *Bottled creamy salad dressings* can top mashed or baked potatoes instead of butter or sour cream; or sauté fresh vegetables with a tablespoon of *vinaigrette dressing* instead of oil. Use *garlic-flavored spreadable cheese* thinned with a little milk to make a sauce for pasta, noodles, or vegetables.

STOCK UP

Keeping your kitchen well stocked with foods you use on a regular basis, will not only cut down your shopping and prepping time, it will ensure that no matter how busy you are, you'll always have the makings of a healthy meal.

Pantry (nonperishables)

Every week or so, check your larder and add to your big shopping list any items that are running low.

- Quick-cooking white and brown rice, couscous, and other quick-cooking grains
- Flavored rice mixes
- Noodles and pasta
- Canned broths and soups, packaged soup mixes
- Canned tomato products: crushed, diced, and sauces
- Canned tuna and salmon
- Canned and dried fruit
- Nuts
- Peanut butter or other nut butters
- Oils: extra-virgin and light olive oils, sesame, and a nut oil
- Dried herbs and spices and herb and spice blends
- Condiments: vinegars, relishes, pickles, chutneys, mustards, ketchup, olives, sun-dried tomatoes, pesto, salsas
- Salad dressings and bottled sauces (steak, soy, peanut, curry, etc.)
- Sweeteners: sugar or sugar substitute, honey, jams
- Onions, garlic, shallots, ginger, potatoes

Refrigerator

Place items that are used most often in the front of the fridge and lesser-used items behind them. Move rear items to the front about every other week, so you remember to use them.

- Fresh meats, fish, and poultry
- Fresh vegetables, chopped produce, and salad fixings
- Fresh pasta (cooks faster than dried)
- Sliced deli meats and whole sausage
- Cheeses: sliced deli cheeses, feta, blue or Gorgonzola, freshly grated Parmesan, and Cheddar
- Milk, yogurt, sour cream
- Butter and cream cheese
- Mayonnaise

- Citrus fruits
- Juices and other beverages

Freezer

Wrap meat and poultry in freezer wrap or heavy-duty foil, pressing out all the air. Label each package with the name of the cut, number of servings, and the date. To freeze seafood, be sure it is very fresh, and wrap in plastic wrap and heavy-duty foil.

- Fresh meat, fish, and poultry that will be used at a later date
- Chopped raw vegetables: onions, carrots, bell peppers, celery, leeks, broccoli, and cauliflower florets
- Packaged frozen vegetables and vegetable combos
- Flash-frozen fruits and berries
- Breads, tortillas, pita pockets
- Leftovers: casseroles, soups, stews, grilled meats, and veggies
- Cooked rice and pasta (freeze in individual containers sized to suit your family)
- Sliced pound cake (to top with fruit or berries, ice cream, or puddings for a quick dessert)

CUT DOWN KITCHEN TIME

This should be the fun part. Get the kids to help out by setting the table, pouring milk, and doing other simple tasks to save you time. Spend a minute or two to organize your work area and have the appropriate tools and cookware at the ready to speed your preparations along.

How Long Will It Keep?

Foods frozen longer than for the recommended times aren't harmful—they just won't be at their peak flavor and texture.

Food (0°F)	Time in Freezer
Milk	3 months
Butter	6 to 9 months
Cheese, hard (Cheddar, Swiss)	6 months
Cheese, soft (Brie, Bel Paese)	6 months
Cream, half-and-half	4 months
Sour cream	don't feeze
Eggs (raw yolks, whites)	1 year
Frankfurters (opened or unopened packages)	1 to 2 months
Luncheon meats (opened or unopened packages)	1 to 2 months
Bacon	1 month
Sausage, raw, links or patties	1 to 2 months
Ham, fully cooked (whole, half, slices)	1 to 2 months
Ground or stew meat	3 to 4 months
Steaks	6 to 12 months
Chops	3 to 6 months
Roasts	4 to 12 months
Chicken or turkey, whole	1 year
Chicken or turkey, pieces	9 months
Casseroles, cooked, poultry	4 to 6 months
Casseroles, cooked, meat	2 to 3 months
Soups and stews	2 to 3 months
Fish, lean (cod, flounder, haddock)	6 months
Fish, fatty (bluefish, mackerel, salmon)	2 to 3 months
Fish, cooked	4 to 6 months
Fish, smoked	2 months in vacuum pack
Shrimp, scallops, squid, shucked clams, mussels, oysters	3 to 6 months
Pizza	1 to 2 months
Breads and rolls, yeast	3 to 6 month
Breads, quick	2 to 3 months
Cakes, unfrosted	3 months
Cheesecakes	2 to 3 months
Cookies, baked	3 months
Cookie dough, raw	2 to 3 months
Pies, fruit, unbaked	8 months
Pies, custard or meringue-topped	don't freeze
Piecrust, raw	2 to 3 months
Nuts, salted	6 to 8 months
Nuts, unsalted	9 to 12 months

Get Organized

- Become familiar with the recipe so you don't have to stop to read each step while you work.
- Clear an adequate workspace with plenty of elbow room.
- Preheat the oven or stovetop grill and fill a pot or kettle with water and leave it to boil before you gather your ingredients.
- Assemble all the ingredients, cookware, and tools so that everything is in easy reach.
- Remove utensils after using; clutter will slow you down.

Useful Utensils

- Knives: a paring knife for trimming veggies and fruits; a chef's knife for fast slicing and chopping; and a serrated knife to cut through delicate foods like bread, tomatoes, and cake
- Heavy 12-inch nonstick skillet with lid, for browning, sautéing, stir-frying, and making sauces
- Heatproof silicone spatulas in a few sizes
- Kitchen scissors for snipping fresh herbs
- Microplane® grater for grating hard cheeses, citrus peels, and ginger

Time-Saving Appliances

- Mini food processor with changeable cutting disks for chopping, slicing, and shredding
- Immersion blender for pureeing soups, making gravies, dips, and sauces
- Microwave oven for defrosting frozen meats, fish, and poultry; precooking potatoes, winter squash, and other ingredients that take a long time to cook; reheating leftovers; steaming vegetables; melting butter and cheese
- Grill pan for fat-free grilling, uses very little oil, preheats fast, and leaves familiar grill marks on the food
- Slow cooker lets you prep, set, and forget, then come home to a hot, homemade dinner at the end of a long day. All you have to do then is set the table.

Shortcuts to Meal Preparation

- Choose lean cuts of meat, such as sirloin, which will cook faster than fattier cuts, such as chuck. Save the tougher cuts for the slow cooker.
- Put up water to boil for noodles, rice, and pasta as soon as you get home. While the water is coming to a boil, brown the meat or sauté onions.
- If using ground beef in a recipe, brown it the previous evening, then let cool, bag, and refrigerate.
- Use your microwave to precook ingredients that normally take a long time to cook, such as potatoes and other root veggies, or add a tablespoon of water to a microwavable bowl, cover, and steam them.
- Cook enough for two meals and turn the leftovers into different dishes later in the week. For example, a pot of chili one night will give you leftovers to make tacos, nachos, or to top baked potatoes.

• Freeze leftovers in individual servings and you'll have a stockpile of quick and healthy meals whenever you want.

• Kids love finger foods. So when you find yourself in a real time crunch, serve wholesome sandwiches, store-bought frozen fish sticks or breaded chicken nuggets, empanadas or calzones. Be sure to include a salad or crudités and a dip (all purchased ready to serve).

Top 10 Slow Cooker Tips

1. Prep the recipe the night before: measure ingredients, cut vegetables, trim meats, mix liquids and seasonings. Refrigerate components separately in zip-tight plastic bags or containers. In the morning add the ingredients into the cooker, turn on the switch, and go about your day.

2. Cut meats and vegetables for soups and stews to the same bite-size pieces to ensure even cooking.

3. Start with the crock at room temperature. Don't use frozen ingredients, which prolong the heating process, increasing the possible growth of harmful bacteria. Thaw meats, poultry, and veggies before adding them to the slow cooker.

4. For richer flavor, dredge meats and poultry in flour and brown in a nonstick skillet before adding them to the slow cooker. Scrape up browned bits and add to the cooker for a heartier sauce.

5. Use flavorful spices and seasonings such as chili powder and garlic sparingly, as slow cooking tends to intensify these flavors. Dried herbs may loose some of their flavor, so adjust seasonings at end of cooking. If using fresh herbs, save some to add at the last minutes for best flavor.

6. Add dairy products such as milk or yogurt during the last hour of cooking to prevent curdling, or use canned evaporated milk.

7. For even cooking, fill slow cooker at least halfway, but never to the brim. Place hard vegetables like turnips and potatoes on the bottom; they cook more slowly than meat. For soups and stews, leave about 2 inches of space below the rim.

8. Always cook covered. Don't lift the lid during the cooking process—it causes steam to escape and reduces the internal temperature. Resist stirring the pot. The flavors will blend automatically as the steam is infused back into the cooking food. Add 20 minutes to the cooking time whenever you lift the lid.

9. If your recipe yields more liquid than you want, remove solids to a serving dish and keep warm. Turn the slow cooker to high and cook the remaining liquid until it is reduced to the desired thickness.

10. To convert a regular recipe, use about half the liquid called for and add more during the last hour of cooking, if needed.

CHAPTER 1

Beef, Veal, Lamb & Pork

Skirt Steak
with Chimichurri Sauce

ACTIVE TIME 15 minutes TOTAL TIME 30 minutes
MAKES 4 servings

In Argentina, where grilled meat is a staple, chimichurri is the accompaniment of choice. This tangy sauce, similar in texture to pesto, also can be used with a variety of other dishes and makes an excellent sandwich spread. If you have any left over, refrigerate it in a container with a tight-fitting lid for up to two days. Bring it to room temperature before serving.

Chimichurri Sauce

1	garlic clove, crushed with garlic press
$1/4$	teaspoon salt
1	cup loosely packed fresh flat-leaf parsley leaves, chopped
1	cup loosely packed fresh cilantro leaves, chopped
2	tablespoons olive oil
1	tablespoon red wine vinegar
$1/4$	teaspoon crushed red pepper

Steak

1	beef skirt steak or flank steak ($1^1/4$ pounds)
$1/4$	teaspoon salt
$1/8$	teaspoon coarsely ground black pepper

1. Prepare sauce: In small bowl, with fork, stir garlic, salt, parsley, cilantro, oil, vinegar, and crushed red pepper until mixed. (Or, in mini food processor or blender, puree sauce ingredients until smooth.) Makes about $1/4$ cup.

2. Prepare grill for covered direct grilling over medium heat.

3. Sprinkle steak with salt and pepper; place on grill over medium heat; cover and grill steak 3 minutes per side for medium-rare or until desired doneness.

4. Transfer steak to cutting board; let stand 10 minutes to set juices for easier slicing. Thinly slice steak crosswise against grain. Serve with chimichurri sauce.

Each serving steak with 1 tablespoon sauce: About 300 calories, 40g protein, 1g carbohydrate, 14g total fat (5g saturated), 121mg cholesterol, 380mg sodium.

Paprika Steak
with Pimiento Salsa

ACTIVE TIME **10 minutes** TOTAL TIME **25 minutes**
MAKES **6 servings**

One of the easiest ways to flavor meat for the grill is to rub it first with spices. For this recipe, we use a simple rub of smoked paprika. If you are partial to one of the excellent commercial spice rubs that are now widely available, by all means feel free to substitute an equal amount. The accompanying sweet-tart salsa will complement almost any flavor combo.

1^1/2   pounds beef skirt steak
1   tablespoon mild smoked Spanish paprika
      or regular paprika
1   teaspoon salt
1   jar (4 ounces) sliced pimientos, drained
1   small garlic clove, crushed with garlic press
^{1}/4   cup blanched almonds, coarsely chopped
2   tablespoons raisins, coarsely chopped
1   tablespoon capers, drained and chopped
1   tablespoon extra-virgin olive oil
1   tablespoon red wine vinegar

1. Prepare grill for direct grilling over medium heat.
2. Rub steak all over with paprika. Sprinkle both sides with salt. Set aside.
3. In small bowl, with fork, stir pimientos, garlic, almonds, raisins, capers, oil, and vinegar. Makes about ^{3}/4 cup salsa.
4. Place steak on grill over medium heat and grill, turning once, 6 to 8 minutes for medium-rare or until desired doneness. Transfer steak to cutting board; let stand 5 minutes to set juices for easier slicing. Thinly slice steak against grain. Serve with salsa.

Each serving steak: About 190 calories, 27g protein, 1g carbohydrate, 8g total fat (3g saturated), 81mg cholesterol, 440mg sodium.

Each tablespoon salsa: About 30 calories, 1g protein, 2g carbohydrate, 2g total fat (0g saturated), 0mg cholesterol, 25mg sodium.

Chile Steak
with Avocado Tomato Salad

TOTAL TIME 30 minutes
MAKES 4 servings

Chile Steak

2	chipotle chiles in adobo, finely chopped
2	garlic cloves, crushed with garlic press
2	tablespoons honey
2	teaspoons fresh lime juice
1	teaspoon dried oregano
3/4	teaspoon salt
1/4	teaspoon coarsely ground black pepper
1	beef skirt steak (1 1/4 pounds)

Avocado Tomato Salad

1	pint red or yellow cherry tomatoes, each cut in half
1	ripe avocado, pitted, peeled, and cut into 3/4-inch pieces
1	tablespoon coarsely chopped fresh cilantro leaves
2	teaspoons fresh lime juice
1/8	teaspoon salt

1. Prepare steak: In cup, with fork, mix chipotles, garlic, honey, and lime juice; set aside.

2. In another cup, mix oregano, salt, and pepper; rub on steak.

3. Heat ridged grill pan over medium-high heat until very hot. Place steak in pan; brush top with half of chipotle mixture and cook 2 minutes. Turn steak; brush with remaining chipotle mixture and cook 2 to 3 minutes longer for medium-rare or until desired doneness. Turn again; cook 30 seconds. Transfer steak to cutting board; keep warm.

4. Meanwhile, prepare salad: In large bowl, combine tomatoes, avocado, cilantro, lime juice, and salt; toss until well mixed and evenly coated with dressing.

5. Thinly slice steak; serve with avocado salad.

Each serving steak: About 310 calories, 35g protein, 13g carbohydrate, 12g total fat (4g saturated), 108mg cholesterol, 865mg sodium.

Each 1/2 cup avocado salad: About 65 calories, 1g protein, 5g carbohydrate, 5g total fat (1g saturated), 0mg cholesterol, 55mg sodium.

This recipe calls for skirt steak, which is a long, flat piece of meat (the diaphragm muscle) that's very flavorful. It is not the tenderest cut of beef, but quick grilling will yield succulent results. It has become the meat used most often for fajitas, the popular southwestern dish. If you can't find skirt steak, flank steak makes a good replacement, just increase cooking time to 6 to 8 minutes per side.

Coriander Steak with Warm Corn Salad

TOTAL TIME 25 minutes
MAKES 4 servings

These steaks are flavored with a rub that contains coriander seeds and black peppercorns that you can easily crush with a mortar and pestle. If you don't own one, place the spices in a sturdy plastic zip-tight bag, seal the bag, and pound the spices several times with a meat mallet or heavy skillet. Measure the peppercorns before using.

2	teaspoons olive oil
1	tablespoon coriander seeds, crushed
1	teaspoon cracked black pepper
3/4	teaspoon salt
2	boneless beef top loin steaks, 3/4 inch thick (10 ounces each)
1	small red pepper, cut into 1/4-inch pieces
1/2	small red onion, finely chopped
2	cups corn kernels cut from cobs (about 4 ears)
1	tablespoon chopped fresh cilantro leaves
1	tablespoon fresh lime juice
1/2	teaspoon ground cumin

1. Heat 10-inch grill pan or cast-iron skillet over medium-high heat until very hot. Brush pan with 1 teaspoon oil. On waxed paper, mix coriander, black pepper, and 1/2 teaspoon salt; use to coat both sides of steaks.

2. Place steaks in pan; cook, turning once, about 8 minutes for medium-rare, or until desired doneness.

3. Meanwhile, in 2-quart saucepan, heat remaining 1 teaspoon oil over medium-high heat. Add red pepper and onion; cook, stirring occasionally, until soft, about 5 minutes. Stir in corn; heat through. Stir in cilantro, lime juice, cumin, and remaining 1/4 teaspoon salt. Makes about 2 1/2 cups.

4. Transfer steak to cutting board. Let stand 5 minutes to set juices for easier slicing. Thinly slice steak and serve with corn salad.

Each serving: About 430 calories, 31g protein, 25g carbohydrate, 25g total fat (9g saturated), 84mg cholesterol, 705mg sodium.

Pan-Fried Steak with Spinach and Tomatoes

TOTAL TIME 30 minutes

MAKES 4 servings

1	large garlic clove, crushed with garlic press
1	teaspoon freshly grated lemon peel
1/2	teaspoon salt
1/2	teaspoon coarsely ground black pepper
2	boneless beef top loin or rib-eye steaks, 3/4 inch thick (10 ounces each), well trimmed
1	teaspoon olive oil
1	teaspoon cornstarch
1/2	cup chicken broth
1	cup grape tomatoes or cherry tomatoes, each cut in half
1	bag (10 ounces) prewashed spinach, tough stems discarded

1. In cup, with fork, stir garlic, lemon peel, salt, and pepper until well blended; use to rub on both sides of steak.

2. In nonstick 12-inch skillet, heat oil over medium heat until very hot. Add steaks and cook 5 to 6 minutes per side for medium-rare or until desired doneness. Transfer steaks to plate; keep warm.

3. In cup, blend cornstarch and broth until smooth. To same skillet, add broth mixture, tomatoes, and spinach. Heat to boiling over medium-high heat; cook, stirring, until spinach wilts, 1 to 2 minutes. Cut each steak in half and serve with spinach mixture.

Each serving: About 350 calories, 30g protein, 3g carbohydrate, 24g total fat (9g saturated), 92mg cholesterol, 540mg sodium.

There's no doubt about it: Grilled steaks are superb. Panfrying steak in a hot skillet also has its virtues: You can use the tasty browned bits of meat clinging to the pan after the steak is removed to make a sauce. In this case, simply add some chicken broth in which you've dissolved cornstarch. And you can cook your vegetables—cherry tomatoes and fresh spinach—in the same pan with the sauce.

Filet Mignon with Horseradish Salsa

TOTAL TIME 30 minutes

MAKES 4 servings

Filet mignon is a boneless cut of beef from the narrow end of the tenderloin. It is highly prized for its extremely tender texture. Because it is so lean, it is not as flavorful as well-marbled beef on the bone. The solution: rub it with seasoning before grilling and serve with a tongue-tingling horseradish-spiked salsa. This salsa goes well with any grilled steak, such as flank steak, skirt steak, or a sirloin cut.

Horseradish Salsa

- 3 ripe medium tomatoes (about 1 pound), each cut into $1/2$-inch pieces
- 1 cup loosely packed fresh parsley leaves, chopped
- $1/2$ small red onion, finely chopped
- 2 tablespoons bottled white horseradish, or more to taste
- 1 tablespoon balsamic vinegar
- 1 tablespoon olive oil
- $1/2$ teaspoon salt

Steak

- 1 teaspoon cracked black pepper
- 1 teaspoon olive oil
- $1/2$ teaspoon salt
- $1/4$ teaspoon dried thyme
- 1 garlic clove, crushed with garlic press
- 4 beef tenderloin steaks (filet mignon), 1 inch thick (6 ounces each)

1. Prepare salsa: In medium bowl, combine tomatoes, parsley, onion, horseradish, vinegar, oil, and salt; toss until well mixed. Cover and refrigerate until serving time. Makes 2 cups.

2. Prepare grill for direct grilling over medium heat.

3. Meanwhile, in cup, with fork, mix pepper, oil, salt, thyme, and garlic; use to rub all over steaks.

4. Place steaks on grill over medium heat and grill, turning once, 10 to 12 minutes for medium-rare or until desired doneness. Serve steaks with salsa.

Each serving steak: About 330 calories, 39g protein, 9g carbohydrate, 15g total fat (4g saturated), 89mg cholesterol, 710mg sodium.

Each $1/4$ cup salsa: About 55 calories, 1g protein, 4g carbohydrate, 2g total fat (0g saturated), 180mg sodium.

Steak au Poivre

TOTAL TIME 25 minutes
MAKES 4 servings

1	tablespoon whole black peppercorns, crushed
$^1/_2$	teaspoon salt
4	beef tenderloin steaks (filet mignon), $1^1/_4$ inches thick (5 ounces each)
1	tablespoon butter or margarine
1	tablespoon olive oil
$^1/_4$	cup dry white wine
2	tablespoons brandy
$^1/_2$	cup heavy or whipping cream
1	tablespoon chopped fresh chives

This French classic couldn't be easier to prepare. First, the steaks have been cooked to the desired doneness in a mixture of butter and olive oil. Then, once the steaks are removed to a warm platter, the luscious sauce is quickly whipped up right in the same pan. If you can't find chives, substitute finely chopped green onions.

1. In cup, with fork, mix peppercorns and salt; use to rub on both sides of steaks.

2. In nonstick 12-inch skillet, melt butter with oil over medium heat. Add steaks and cook 7 to 8 minutes per side for medium-rare or until desired doneness. Transfer steaks to dinner plates; keep warm.

3. Add wine and brandy to skillet; heat to boiling, stirring, until browned bits are loosened from bottom of skillet. Add cream and boil until sauce has thickened, about 1 minute. Stir in chives. Pour sauce over steaks.

Each serving: About 579 calories, 26g protein, 2g carbohydrate, 50g total fat (22g saturated), 149mg cholesterol, 399mg sodium.

Mongolian Beef Stir-fry

TOTAL TIME 30 minutes
MAKES 4 servings

This mouth-watering stir-fry gets its sweet-hot flavor from bottled hoisin sauce, a Chinese staple. A mixture of soybeans, garlic, chile peppers, and spices, hoisin is used to flavor innumerable dishes. It can be found in the Asian food section of most supermarkets and in Asian markets. Tightly closed, hoisin will keep indefinitely in the refrigerator.

1	beef flank steak (1 pound) thinly sliced
1	tablespoon cornstarch
1	tablespoon grated, peeled fresh ginger
4	tablespoons soy sauce
2	tablespoons vegetable oil
1	medium onion, thinly sliced
1	medium red pepper, thinly sliced
2	bunches green onions, cut into 3-inch pieces
2	garlic cloves, thinly sliced
2	tablespoons dry sherry
2	tablespoons hoisin sauce
1	teaspoon sugar
$1/8$	teaspoon crushed red pepper

1. In large bowl, toss steak with cornstarch, ginger, and 2 table-spoons soy sauce until evenly coated; set aside.

2. In nonstick 12-inch skillet, heat 1 tablespoon oil over medium heat until very hot. Add onion, red pepper, green onions, and garlic; cook, stirring frequently (stir-frying), until vegetables are tender-crisp, 5 minutes.

3. Meanwhile, in cup, with fork, mix sherry, hoisin, sugar, crushed red pepper, and remaining 2 tablespoons soy sauce until blended.

4. Transfer vegetables to bowl. In same skillet, heat remaining 1 tablespoon oil over medium heat. Add beef mixture; stir-fry until lightly browned, about 2 minutes. Stir in sherry mixture; heat to boiling. Return vegetables to skillet; heat through.

Each serving: About 360 calories, 26g protein, 20g carbohydrate, 19g total fat (6g saturated), 59mg cholesterol, 1205mg sodium.

Chili-Crusted Flank Steak

TOTAL TIME 30 minutes

MAKES 6 servings

2	tablespoons chili powder
1	tablespoon brown sugar
1/4	teaspoon salt
2	tablespoons fresh lime juice
1	large garlic clove, crushed with garlic press
1	beef flank steak (1 1/2 pounds)
3	large red onions (8 ounces each), each cut into 6 wedges
1	tablespoon olive oil

1. Prepare grill for direct grilling over medium heat.

2. Meanwhile, in cup, with fork, stir chili powder, sugar, salt, lime juice, and garlic until blended. Use to rub on both sides of steak. In medium bowl, toss red onions with oil.

3. Place steak and onions on grill over medium heat and grill steak, turning once, 15 to 20 minutes for medium-rare or until desired doneness. Cook onions, turning occasionally, until browned and just tender, about 15 minutes.

4. Transfer onions and steak to cutting board. Let steak stand 10 minutes to set juices for easier slicing. Thinly slice steak and serve with grilled onions.

Each serving: About 270 calories, 24g protein, 15g carbohydrate, 13g total fat (5g saturated), 57mg cholesterol, 200mg sodium.

Heed the heat. Chili powder, a blend of garlic, oregano, cumin, coriander, cloves, and ground dried chiles, ranges in flavor and hotness depending on the brand, so adjust the amount to your taste. Two tablespoons is the average; some people prefer more heat than others.

Stir-fried Steak and Vegetables

TOTAL TIME 25 minutes
MAKES 4 servings

1	beef top round steak (1 pound)
1/3	cup reduced-sodium soy sauce
2	large garlic cloves, crushed with garlic press
1	medium onion
1	red pepper
2	teaspoons vegetable oil
1	package (8 ounces) sliced cremini mushrooms
1	bag (16 ounces) fresh vegetables for stir-frying (such as broccoli, carrots, snow peas)
2	tablespoons grated, peeled fresh ginger
3/4	cup water
1	pouch (8 1/2 ounces) precooked brown rice, heated as label directs

Here's the trick to cut raw beef into thin, even slices for stir-fries: Freeze the beef first for about fifteen minutes until it is firm. Then proceed slicing with a sharp knife. By the time you finish, the meat will have lost its chill and you can proceed with the recipe as directed.

1. With knife held in slanting position, almost parallel to cutting surface, cut round steak crosswise into 1/8-inch-thick slices. In medium bowl, toss steak slices with 1 tablespoon soy sauce and 1 crushed garlic clove. Let stand 5 minutes.

2. Meanwhile, cut onion in half, then cut crosswise into thin slices. Cut red pepper into 1/4-inch-thick slices. Set vegetables aside.

3. In deep nonstick 12-inch skillet, heat 1 teaspoon oil over medium heat until very hot but not smoking. Add half of beef and stir frequently (stir-fry) just until beef is no longer pink, 30 to 45 seconds. Transfer beef to plate. Repeat with remaining beef, without adding additional oil.

4. In same skillet, heat remaining 1 teaspoon oil until hot. Add mushrooms and onion; cover and cook, stirring occasionally, until mushrooms are browned, 3 to 4 minutes.

5. Add vegetables for stir-frying, red pepper, ginger, water, and remaining soy sauce and garlic to skillet. Stir-fry until vegetables are tender-crisp, 5 to 6 minutes. Remove skillet from heat; stir in beef with its juices. Serve over rice.

Each serving: About 380 calories, 34g protein, 34g carbohydrate, 12g total fat (4g saturated), 68mg cholesterol, 790mg sodium.

Beef Tamale Pie

TOTAL TIME 25 minutes
MAKES 4 servings

In this version of the popular southwestern dish, the crust is made of sliced precooked polenta (cornmeal) placed on top of, rather than underneath, the savory filling for less fuss and quicker cooking. If you can't find canned diced tomatoes with green chiles, use regular canned diced tomatoes and add your own chiles.

1   log (16 ounces) precooked polenta, cut crosswise into 8 slices
1   package (17 ounces) fully cooked roast beef au jus
1   can (14$^1/_2$ ounces) diced tomatoes with green chiles
2   teaspoons chili powder
$^1/_2$ cup loosely packed fresh cilantro leaves
1   cup frozen whole-kernel corn
1   cup shredded Mexican cheese blend (from 8-ounce package)

1. Preheat broiler. Arrange polenta slices in single layer on cookie sheet. Place cookie sheet in broiling pan. Broil at closest position to heat source until polenta is golden on top, 10 to 12 minutes.
2. Meanwhile, drain beef jus into nonstick 12-inch skillet. Add tomatoes with their juice and chili powder; heat to boiling over high heat. Boil until sauce has thickened, 4 to 5 minutes.
3. While mixture boils, shred beef with two forks and coarsely chop cilantro.
4. Stir frozen corn and shredded beef into tomato mixture; heat through. Remove skillet from heat. Stir in all but 1 teaspoon cilantro.
5. Arrange polenta over beef mixture; sprinkle with cheese and remaining cilantro. Cover skillet and let stand until cheese melts, about 2 minutes.

Each serving: About 380 calories, 30g protein, 34g carbohydrate, 14g total fat (8g saturated), 97mg cholesterol, 1,800mg sodium.

Spicy Beef with Couscous

TOTAL TIME 30 minutes

MAKES 4 servings

1	tablespoon vegetable oil
1	medium onion, chopped
1	garlic clove, crushed with garlic press
1	teaspoon minced, peeled fresh ginger
1	pound lean (90%) ground beef
1	tablespoon curry powder
1	teaspoon garam masala spice mix
1/2	teaspoon salt
1	small yellow summer squash (6 ounces), cut into 1/2-inch pieces
1	cup chicken broth
1	cup frozen peas
1/2	cup loosely packed fresh cilantro leaves, chopped
1	cup plain couscous (Moroccan pasta)
1/3	cup golden raisins

1. In nonstick 12-inch skillet, heat oil over medium heat. Add onion and cook, stirring, until golden, about 3 minutes. Stir in garlic and ginger; cook 1 minute.

2. Stir in ground beef and cook, breaking up meat with side of spoon, until meat is no longer pink, about 5 minutes. Stir in curry powder, garam masala, and salt; cook 30 seconds. Add squash and cook 2 minutes. Add broth and frozen peas; cook until thickened slightly. Stir in cilantro.

3. Meanwhile, prepare couscous as label directs but add raisins to water.

4. Fluff couscous with fork and serve with beef mixture.

Each serving: About 520 calories, 34g protein, 57g carbohydrate, 16g total fat (5g saturated), 69mg cholesterol, 650mg sodium.

In addition to curry powder, this fragrant dish is flavored with *garam masala*, a blend of dry-roasted, ground spices that can include black pepper, cinnamon, cloves, coriander, cumin, cardamom, and dried chiles. Look for *garam masala* in Indian markets and in the spice section of some supermarkets. Before adding the cilantro, taste to check the heat level of the curry. If you prefer it hotter, add a drop or two of hot pepper sauce.

Upside-down Shepherd's Pie

TOTAL TIME 20 minutes

MAKES 4 servings

Shepherd's Pie was originally concocted as a way to use up the leftovers from Sunday dinner, but thanks to ground beef and packaged refrigerated mashed potatoes, the prep time for this recipe has been slashed to a bare minimum. For a change of pace, replace half of the mashed potatoes with an equal amount of cooked mashed parsnips or carrots.

1	package (20 ounces) refrigerated mashed potatoes
1	pound lean (90%) ground beef
1	tablespoon butter or margarine
1	cup chopped onion
1/3	cup ketchup
1	teaspoon dillweed
1/2	cup loosely packed fresh parsley leaves, chopped
1/3	cup reduced-fat sour cream

1. Preheat oven to 450°F. Spray 1 1/2-quart baking dish or deep-dish pie plate with nonstick cooking spray. Press potatoes onto bottom and up side of dish. Bake potato crust until edge is golden, about 20 minutes.

2. Meanwhile, heat 10-inch skillet over medium-high heat until very hot. Add ground beef and cook, breaking meat up with side of spoon, until meat is no longer pink, 4 to 5 minutes. Spoon beef into paper-towel-lined bowl to drain.

3. In skillet, melt butter over medium heat. Add onion and cook, stirring occasionally, until tender and golden, 6 to 7 minutes.

4. Return beef to skillet with onion. Stir in ketchup and dillweed. Reduce heat to low; stir in parsley and sour cream. To serve, spoon ground-beef mixture into mashed-potato crust.

Each serving: About 490 calories, 26g protein, 31g carbohydrate, 29g total fat (12g saturated), 94mg cholesterol, 945mg sodium.

Everybody has his or her own idea of what constitutes the perfect burger. This one is ours. We serve it on a lightly toasted bun with lettuce, tomato, and grilled Vidalia or Maui onion, both of which are prized for being among the sweetest and juiciest in the market. Also recommended is the Oso Sweet onion, which has almost 50 percent more sugar than the Vidalia. If you are partial to the red onion, by all means go for it.

The Perfect Burger

TOTAL TIME 25 minutes
MAKES 4 servings

1¼ pounds ground beef chuck
1   teaspoon salt
½   teaspoon coarsely ground black pepper
1   large sweet onion, such as Vidalia or Maui, cut into
       ½-inch-thick rounds
4   hamburger buns, split
4   green-leaf lettuce leaves
2   ripe medium tomatoes, each thinly sliced

1. Prepare grill for direct grilling over medium heat or preheat ridged grill pan over medium heat until very hot.

2. Shape ground beef into 4 patties, handling meat as little as possible. Sprinkle ¾ teaspoon salt and the pepper on both sides of patties. Thread one metal skewer horizontally through center of each onion slice. Sprinkle onion slices with remaining ¼ teaspoon salt.

3. Place burgers and onion slices on hot grill over medium heat and grill, turning once, 8 to 10 minutes for medium-rare or until desired doneness. Onions should be browned and tender.

4. About 1 minute before burgers are done, add buns to grill, cut sides down, to grill and grill just until toasted. Serve burgers on buns with lettuce, tomato, and onion.

Each serving: About 485 calories, 31g protein, 33g carbohydrate, 25g total fat (9g saturated), 96mg cholesterol, 920mg sodium.

CREAMY BURGER TOPPINGS

Nowadays, there is a wide variety of commercially prepared sauces, salsas, and condiments available in almost every supermarket, but, of course, nothing beats homemade. So, if you want to offer something a little more special than mustard, relish, and ketchup, here are three tasty mayonnaise-based toppings you can whip up in just a few minutes. If you can't decide on which one to serve, prepare all three.

Onion-Thyme Mayo

Place **1 medium onion,** cut crosswise into $1/2$-inch-thick rounds, on grill over medium heat and grill, turning once, until tender and browned on both sides, 8 to 10 minutes. Transfer onion to cutting board; coarsely chop. Place onion in small serving bowl. Add $1/4$ **cup light mayonnaise** and **1 teaspoon fresh thyme leaves,** chopped; stir until blended. Makes about $1/2$ cup.

Each tablespoon: About 30 calories, 0g protein, 2g carbohydrate, 3g total fat (1g saturated), 3mg cholesterol, 60mg sodium.

Horseradish-Mustard Mayo

In small serving bowl, combine $1/4$ **cup light mayonnaise, 1 tablespoon undrained bottled white horseradish,** and **2 teaspoons Dijon mustard with seeds;** stir until blended. Makes about $1/3$ cup.

Each tablespoon: About 45 calories, 0g protein, 1g carbohydrate, 4g total fat (1g saturated), 4mg cholesterol, 105mg sodium.

Bacon-Chipotle Mayo

Place **2 slices bacon** on paper-towel-lined microwave-safe plate. Cover with paper towel and cook in microwave oven on High until well browned, $1^1/2$ to 2 minutes. Set aside until cool and crisp, then crumble bacon into small serving bowl. Add $1/4$ **cup light mayonnaise** and **1 teaspoon puree** from canned chipotle chile in adobo; stir until blended. Makes about $1/3$ cup.

Each tablespoon: About 55 calories, 1g protein, 1g carbohydrate, 5g total fat (1g saturated), 6mg cholesterol, 135mg sodium.

Mini Burgers

TOTAL TIME 25 minutes
MAKES 12 mini burgers

Bigger is not necessarily better these days, especially when it comes to weight control. Even restaurants that pride themselves on their generous servings now also feature options like these delicious little burgers to help diners control their portion size. Each of these minis offers a different but equally tasty flavor experience. Served with one of the Creamy Burger Toppings, these minis will deliver so much flavor that no one will even think about size. Choose your favorite seasoning, or if you're feeding a crowd, prepare some of each and let guests choose for themselves.

1 1/4	pounds ground beef chuck
3/4	teaspoon salt
1/2	teaspoon freshly ground black pepper
12	mini potato rolls, mini pitas, or other small buns
	plum tomato slices, small lettuce leaves, dill pickle slices, and/or onion slices (optional)
	choice of Creamy Burger Toppings (page 37)

1. Prepare grill for direct grilling over medium heat.

2. Shape beef into twelve 1/2-inch-thick mini burgers, handling meat as little as possible. Sprinkle both sides of burgers with salt and pepper.

3. Place mini burgers on hot grill over medium heat and grill, turning once, 5 to 6 minutes for medium or until desired doneness.

4. Serve burgers on rolls with tomato, lettuce, pickles, onion, and topping, if you like.

Each mini burger with roll: About 145 calories, 10g protein, 9g carbohydrate, 8g total fat (3g saturated), 32mg cholesterol, 240mg sodium.

Teriyaki Burgers

Prepare as directed with ground beef, pork, chicken, or turkey, but in Step 2, before shaping burgers, mix **1/2 cup finely chopped water chestnuts, 1/4 cup teriyaki sauce,** and **1/4 teaspoon crushed red pepper** with meat just until well blended but not overmixed. Do not sprinkle burgers with salt and pepper. In Step 4, spoon **1 tablespoon hoisin sauce** over each burger before serving.

Each mini burger with roll: About 165 calories, 11g protein, 13g carbohydrate, 8g total fat (3g saturated), 32mg cholesterol, 410mg sodium.

Pesto Burgers

Prepare as directed with ground chicken, turkey, pork, or beef, but in Step 2, before shaping burgers, mix **¼ cup store-bought pesto** with meat just until well blended but not overmixed. Sprinkle burgers with salt and pepper. Serve burgers as in Step 4 with additional pesto on the side, if you like.

Each mini burger with roll: About 140 calories, 10g protein, 9g carbohydrate, 7g total fat (0g saturated), 1mg cholesterol, 270mg sodium.

Rosemary-Cabernet Burgers

Prepare as directed with ground beef or lamb, but in Step 2, before shaping burgers, mix **⅓ cup Cabernet Sauvignon** or other dry red wine and **2 teaspoons finely chopped rosemary** with meat just until well blended, but not overmixed. Sprinkle burgers with salt and pepper. Serve burgers as in Step 4.

Each mini burger with roll: About 145 calories, 11g protein, 9g carbohydrate, 8g total fat (3g saturated), 32mg cholesterol, 240mg sodium.

Pastrami-Style Burgers

TOTAL TIME 20 minutes
MAKES 4 servings

To mock pastrami sandwiches, ground beef seasoned with coriander, paprika, ginger, and red pepper is grilled and served on rye bread with mustard. If you like, add a slice of Swiss cheese and some well-drained sauerkraut to each burger.

2	teaspoons ground coriander
2	teaspoons paprika
$1^{1}/_{2}$	teaspoons ground ginger
$^{1}/_{2}$	teaspoon sugar
$^{1}/_{4}$	teaspoon ground red pepper (cayenne)
1	teaspoon salt
2	teaspoons coarsely ground black pepper
$1^{1}/_{4}$	pounds ground beef chuck
8	oval slices rye bread with caraway seeds
	deli mustard

1. Prepare grill for direct grilling over medium heat.

2. In cup, with fork, stir coriander, paprika, ginger, sugar, ground red pepper, salt, and black pepper until blended.

3. Shape ground beef into four $^{1}/_{2}$-inch-thick oval burgers, handling meat as little as possible. Place burgers on waxed paper; pat spice mixture onto both sides of burgers.

4. Place burgers on grill over medium heat and grill, turning once, 8 to 9 minutes for medium or until desired doneness. Serve burgers on rye bread with mustard.

Each serving: About 485 calories, 31g protein, 33g carbohydrate, 24g total fat (9g saturated), 96mg cholesterol, 1,095mg sodium.

BLT Burgers (Pictured on page 16)

TOTAL TIME 25 minutes
MAKES 4 servings

$1/2$ cup ketchup
$1/4$ cup light mayonnaise
  1   tablespoon yellow mustard
$1^1/4$ pounds ground beef chuck
  8   slices bacon
  4   sesame-seed buns, split and toasted
       sweet onion slices, tomato slices, and
            romaine lettuce leaves

1. Prepare grill for direct grilling over medium heat.

2. In bowl, with fork, stir ketchup, mayonnaise, and mustard until blended; set sauce aside. Makes about $1/2$ cup.

3. Shape ground beef into four $3/4$-inch-thick burgers, handling meat as little as possible. Wrap each burger with 2 strips bacon, perpendicular to each other.

4. Place burgers on grill over medium heat and grill, turning once, 10 to 12 minutes for medium or until desired doneness.

5. Serve burgers on buns with onion, tomato, lettuce, and sauce.

Each serving: About 575 calories, 34g protein, 27g carbohydrate, 36g total fat (12g saturated), 111mg cholesterol, 870mg sodium.

Jazz up the classic burger with this all-American combo—the burger and the BLT. This recipe also works well with ground chicken. Just add salt and pepper, about $1/4$ teaspoon of each, before shaping the meat into burgers.

41

Blue-and-Black Burgers

TOTAL TIME 30 minutes
MAKES 4 servings

The burger gets Continental treatment here: It is stuffed with blue cheese and served on a brioche roll. Brioche is a light but rich egg-and-butter French yeast bread that comes in large round loaves or buns, perfect for absorbing meat juices and melted cheese. If you can't find brioche rolls, try thick slices of challah bread or opt for a Kaiser roll.

2	tablespoons olive oil
2	tablespoons chopped fresh basil leaves
4	brioche rolls, split
1$\frac{1}{4}$	pounds ground beef chuck
4	ounces blue cheese, divided into four 1-inch pieces
$\frac{3}{4}$	teaspoon salt
1	tablespoon coarsely ground black pepper
4	thin slices sweet onion

1. Prepare grill for direct grilling over medium heat.

2. Meanwhile, in cup, combine oil and basil. Brush oil on one cut side of each roll; set rolls aside.

3. Shape ground beef into 4 balls, handling meat as little as possible. Make indentation in center of each ball; place 1 piece blue cheese in each indentation. Shape meat around cheese; flatten each into 1$\frac{1}{2}$-inch-thick patty. Sprinkle both sides of burgers with salt and pepper to season.

4. Place burgers on grill over medium heat and grill, turning once, 14 to 16 minutes for medium or until desired doneness.

5. During last 2 minutes of grilling burgers, place rolls, cut sides down, on grill rack with burgers and grill until lightly toasted. Serve burgers on rolls with onions.

Each serving: About 745 calories, 40g protein, 39g carbohydrate, 47g total fat (17g saturated), 190mg cholesterol, 1,235mg sodium.

Gingered Pork Burgers

TOTAL TIME 25 minutes
MAKES 4 servings

1/4	cup light mayonnaise
1	tablespoon soy sauce
1 1/4	pounds ground pork or chicken
1/2	cup loosely packed fresh cilantro leaves, coarsely chopped
3	green onions, chopped
1	tablespoon dry sherry
1	tablespoon finely chopped, peeled fresh ginger
1	teaspoon Asian sesame oil
1/4	teaspoon crushed red pepper
3/4	teaspoon salt
4	sesame-seed hamburger buns, split and toasted

Reminiscent of Peking-style pork dumpling flavors, these Asian-spiced ground pork burgers, are served with soy sauce–flavored mayonnaise. If you prefer, you can use ground chicken instead of pork, but if you do, spray the burgers with non-stick cooking spray before placing them on the grill rack.

1. Prepare grill for direct grilling over medium heat.

2. In cup, with fork, stir mayonnaise and soy sauce until blended; set aside. Makes about 1/4 cup.

3. In medium bowl, combine pork, cilantro, green onions, sherry, ginger, sesame oil, crushed red pepper, and salt until blended but not overmixed. Shape pork mixture into four 3/4-inch-thick burgers, handling meat as little as possible.

4. Place burgers on grill over medium heat and grill, turning once, 10 to 12 minutes for medium or until desired doneness. (If using chicken, spray burgers with nonstick cooking spray and grill 12 to 14 minutes.)

5. Serve burgers on buns with soy mayonnaise.

Each serving: About 475 calories, 32g protein, 25g carbohydrate, 26g total fat (8g saturated), 106mg cholesterol, 1,120mg sodium.

Greek Lamb Burgers

TOTAL TIME 25 minutes

MAKES 4 servings

Grilling is a great way to cook juicy and flavorful ground lamb. For extra texture, add some chopped walnuts to the meat just until blended (do not overmix). If you can't find ground lamb at the supermarket, you can make these burgers with ground beef or poultry.

Yogurt Sauce

1	plum tomato, chopped
1/4	cup plain low-fat yogurt
2	tablespoons light mayonnaise
3/4	cup loosely packed fresh mint leaves, coarsely chopped
1/4	teaspoon salt
1/4	teaspoon freshly ground black pepper

Lamb Burgers

1 1/4	pounds ground lamb
1/4	cup walnuts, chopped (optional)
1	garlic clove, crushed with garlic press
2	teaspoons ground cumin
3/4	teaspoon salt
4	(6-inch) pita breads
1	medium Kirby (pickling) cucumber, not peeled, and sliced

1. Prepare grill for direct grilling over medium heat.

2. Prepare sauce: In small bowl, stir tomato, yogurt, mayonnaise, 2 tablespoons mint, salt, and pepper until blended; set aside. Makes about 3/4 cup.

3. Prepare burgers: In medium bowl, combine lamb, walnuts, if using, garlic, cumin, salt, and remaining mint just until blended but not overmixed.

4. Shape lamb mixture into four 3/4-inch-thick burgers, handling meat as little as possible.

5. Place burgers on grill over medium heat and grill, turning once, 10 to 12 minutes for medium or until desired doneness.

6. To serve, cut off one-third from side of each pita. Place burgers in pitas; top with sauce and cucumber.

Each serving: About 485 calories, 32g protein, 31g carbohydrate, 25g total fat (10g saturated), 105mg cholesterol, 985mg sodium.

Sopressata and Roma Bean Salad with Pecorino

TOTAL TIME 20 minutes
MAKES 4 servings

1¼	pounds Roma (Italian) beans or green beans, trimmed
1	lemon
2	tablespoons extra-virgin olive oil
¼	teaspoon salt
⅛	teaspoon coarsely ground black pepper
1	wedge Pecorino Romano cheese (2 ounces)
4	ounces thinly sliced sopressata or Genoa salami, cut into ½-inch-wide strips
2	bunches arugula (4 ounces each), trimmed

1. If Roma beans are very long, cut crosswise into 2½-inch pieces. In 12-inch skillet, heat *1 inch water* to boiling over high heat. Add beans; heat to boiling. Reduce heat to low; simmer until beans are tender-crisp, 6 to 8 minutes. Drain beans. Rinse with cold running water to stop cooking; drain again.

2. Meanwhile, from lemon, grate ½ teaspoon peel and squeeze 2 tablespoons juice. In large bowl, with wire whisk, mix lemon peel and juice with oil, salt, and pepper. With vegetable peeler, shave thin strips from wedge of Pecorino Romano; set aside.

3. Add beans, sopressata, and arugula to dressing in bowl; toss to coat. To serve, spoon salad onto platter and top salad with cheese strips.

Each serving: About 280 calories, 14g protein, 14g carbohydrate, 21g total fat (7g saturated), 41mg cholesterol, 845mg sodium.

Roma beans, which are also known as Italian beans, are slightly broader than regular green beans and have flatter pods. They are a bit chewier and more flavorful, perfect for using in salads. To preserve the lovely texture of this salad, be sure to cook the beans just until crisp-tender and then plunge them into a bowl of ice water right after draining them. This extra step will also keep them bright green.

No-Cook Thai Beef Salad

TOTAL TIME 15 minutes

MAKES 4 servings

Crisp and delicious, this quick salad gets its flavor from classic Thai ingredients: limes, fish sauce, and cilantro. For a little extra bite, substitute trimmed watercress or baby arugula for half of the romaine salad mix.

2 limes

3 tablespoons reduced-sodium Asian fish sauce (nam pla or nuoc nam)

1 tablespoon sugar

1 bag (10 ounces) romaine salad mix

1 seedless cucumber, cut lengthwise in half, then thinly sliced crosswise

8 ounces deli-sliced rare roast beef, cut crosswise into $1/2$-inch-wide strips

1 cup packed fresh cilantro or mint leaves

$1/2$ medium red onion, thinly sliced

1. From limes, grate 1 teaspoon peel and squeeze 3 tablespoons juice.

2. Prepare dressing: In large bowl, with wire whisk, mix lime peel and juice, fish sauce, and sugar until sugar has completely dissolved.

3. Add salad mix, cucumber, roast beef, cilantro, and onion to bowl and toss until well mixed and coated with dressing.

Each serving: About 105 calories, 13g protein, 9g carbohydrate, 2g total fat (1g saturated), 26mg cholesterol, 485mg sodium.

Veal Scaloppine Marsala

TOTAL TIME 25 minutes

MAKES 6 servings

The purpose of pounding veal cutlets for this Italian favorite is twofold: It tenderizes the meat and ensures even cooking. Another tip for success: make sure the skillet is hot (but not so hot that it will burn the butter), and don't overcook the meat. Serve with rice or crusty bread and some simply steamed green beans.

    1 pound veal cutlets
$1/4$ cup all-purpose flour
$1/4$ teaspoon salt
$1/8$ teaspoon coarsely ground black pepper
    3 tablespoons butter or margarine
$1/2$ cup dry Marsala wine
$1/2$ cup chicken broth
    1 tablespoon chopped fresh parsley

1. With meat mallet, or between two sheets of plastic wrap or waxed paper with rolling pin, pound cutlets to even $1/8$-inch thickness. Cut cutlets into 3" by 3" pieces. On waxed paper, combine flour, salt, and pepper; use to coat both sides of veal, shaking off excess.

2. In nonstick 10-inch skillet, melt butter over medium heat. Cook veal, in batches, until lightly browned, 45 to 60 seconds per side, using slotted spatula to transfer pieces to warm platter as they are browned; keep warm.

3. Stir Marsala and broth into veal drippings in pan; cook until syrupy, 4 to 5 minutes, stirring until browned bits are loosened from bottom of skillet. Pour sauce over veal and sprinkle with parsley.

Each serving: About 179 calories, 17g protein, 5g carbohydrate, 7g total fat (4g saturated), 75mg cholesterol, 288mg sodium.

Summer Squash, Ham, and Mozzarella Crepes

ACTIVE TIME 20 minutes   TOTAL TIME 30 minutes
MAKES 4 servings

2 teaspoons olive oil
1 garlic clove, crushed with garlic press
1 pound plum tomatoes, seeded and chopped
3 zucchini (8 ounces each), each cut lengthwise in half, then crosswise into $1/4$-inch-thick slices
1 small red pepper, thinly sliced
$1/2$ cup loosely packed fresh basil leaves, thinly sliced
$1/2$ teaspoon salt
$1/4$ teaspoon coarsely ground black pepper
1 package ($4^1/2$ ounces) refrigerated crepes (ten 7-inch crepes)
10 thin slices baked ham (6 ounces)
$1^1/2$ cups shredded part-skim mozzarella cheese (6 ounces)

1. Preheat oven to 400°F. In nonstick 12-inch skillet, heat oil over medium heat. Add garlic; cook, stirring, 1 minute. Add tomatoes, zucchini, and red pepper; cover and cook, stirring occasionally, until tender, about 7 minutes.

2. Stir in basil, salt, and pepper; cook, uncovered, until all liquid has evaporated, about 5 minutes. Reserve 1 cup zucchini mixture; keep warm.

3. Place crepes on work surface. Top each crepe with 1 ham slice and then about $1/3$ cup zucchini mixture; sprinkle with mozzarella. Fold each crepe over to enclose filling. Place crepes, seam side up, in two 13" by 9" baking pans. Bake crepes until golden, about 6 minutes. To serve, top with reserved zucchini mixture.

Each serving: About 305 calories, 23g protein, 27g carbohydrate, 13g total fat (5g saturated), 57mg cholesterol, 1,160mg sodium.

Light but satisfying, this dish is a great way to get your family to eat their vegetables. The filling is especially tasty with sun-ripened summer tomatoes, but you can also use well-drained canned peeled plum tomatoes. If you can't find refrigerated crepes, just substitute small flour tortillas.

Ham Steak
with Pineapple Salad

TOTAL TIME 30 minutes

MAKES 4 servings

Asparagus is often available year-round, but the prime season is February through June. If asparagus is unavailable, substitute 1 pound of packaged broccoli florets and proceed as directed in the recipe.

8   small new potatoes, not peeled, each cut in half

1   small bunch (1 pound) asparagus, trimmed

$1/2$ refrigerated cored and peeled pineapple, cut into $1/2$-inch pieces

$1/4$ cup loosely packed fresh cilantro leaves, chopped

1   fully cooked smoked-ham center slice, $1/2$ inch thick ($1^{1/4}$ pounds)

2   tablespoons brown sugar

1   teaspoon chili powder

1. Place vegetable steamer in 10-inch skillet. Add enough *water* to come to just below steamer. Place potatoes in steamer; cover and steam 8 minutes. Place asparagus on top of potatoes and steam until vegetables are tender-crisp, about 5 minutes longer.

2. Meanwhile, in medium serving bowl, toss pineapple and cilantro; set aside.

3. Heat nonstick 12-inch skillet over medium heat until hot. Pat ham dry with paper towels. Rub both sides of ham with sugar and chili powder. Add ham to skillet; cook, turning once, until heated through and glazed, about 5 minutes. Transfer ham to platter; serve with pineapple salad, potatoes, and asparagus.

Each serving: About 300 calories, 29g protein, 33g carbohydrate, 6g total fat (1g saturated), 75mg cholesterol, 1,890mg sodium.

Spiced Pork Tenderloin with Mango Salsa

TOTAL TIME 30 minutes
MAKES 8 servings

Mango Salsa
- 2 ripe medium mangoes, peeled, pitted, and coarsely chopped
- 2 medium kiwifruit, peeled and coarsely chopped
- 3 tablespoons seasoned rice vinegar
- 1 tablespoon grated, peeled fresh ginger
- 1 tablespoon finely chopped fresh cilantro leaves

Pork
- 2 pork tenderloins (1 pound each), trimmed
- 3 tablespoons all-purpose flour
- 1 teaspoon salt
- 1 teaspoon ground cumin
- 1 teaspoon ground coriander
- 1/2 teaspoon ground cinnamon
- 1/2 teaspoon ground ginger

1. Prepare salsa: In medium bowl, combine mangoes, kiwifruit, rice vinegar, ginger, and cilantro; toss until well mixed. Cover and refrigerate if not serving right away. Makes about 4 cups.

2. Prepare grill for direct grilling over medium heat.

3. Holding knife parallel to cutting surface and against long side of pork, cut each tenderloin lengthwise almost in half, being careful not to cut all the way through. Open and spread flat like a book. With meat mallet, or between two sheets of plastic wrap or waxed paper with rolling pin, pound pork to even 1/4-inch thickness. Cut each tenderloin into 4 pieces.

4. On waxed paper, mix flour, salt, cumin, coriander, cinnamon, and ginger; use to coat pork.

5. Place pork on grill over medium heat and grill, turning once, until lightly browned on both sides and pork just loses its pink color throughout, 6 to 7 minutes. Serve with mango salsa.

Each serving with 1/2 cup salsa: About 265 calories, 23g protein, 27g carbohydrate, 6g total fat (2g saturated), 71mg cholesterol, 575mg sodium.

Pork cutlets cut from the tenderloin are pounded thin and coated in an aromatic spice mixture before they are quickly grilled and then served with a lively mango and kiwifruit salsa. If fresh mangoes are unavailable, substitute chopped pitted fresh cherries, nectarines, pears, plums, or tomatoes and a diced yellow pepper for the mangoes and kiwifruit.

Pork Steak with Plum Glaze

TOTAL TIME 30 minutes

MAKES 4 servings

For this recipe we butterfly pork tenderloin (cut it nearly all the way through so that it can be opened to lie almost flat like a book), then pound it for quick, even cooking. This technique is also used to prepare meat for stuffing, rolling, and tying before cooking. A meat mallet is a handy tool for this job, but a small heavy skillet or a rolling pin will work in a pinch.

1	pork tenderloin (1 pound), trimmed
1	teaspoon salt
$1/4$	teaspoon coarsely ground black pepper
$1/2$	cup plum jam or preserves
1	tablespoon brown sugar
1	tablespoon grated, peeled fresh ginger
1	tablespoon fresh lemon juice
$1/2$	teaspoon ground cinnamon or Chinese five-spice powder
2	garlic cloves, crushed with garlic press
4	large plums (1 pound), each cut in half and pitted cooked white rice (optional)

1. Prepare grill for covered direct grilling over medium heat, or preheat ridged grill pan over medium heat until very hot.

2. Holding knife parallel to cutting surface and against long side of tenderloin, cut pork lengthwise almost in half, being careful not to cut all the way through. Open tenderloin and spread flat like a book. With meat mallet, or between two sheets of plastic wrap or waxed paper with rolling pin, pound pork to even $1/4$-inch thickness. Cut tenderloin crosswise into 4 steaks; season with salt and pepper.

3. In small bowl, with fork, mix jam, sugar, ginger, lemon juice, cinnamon, and garlic. Brush one side of each pork steak and cut side of each plum half with plum glaze.

4. Place steaks and plums, glaze side down, on grill over medium heat. Cover and cook 3 minutes. Brush steaks and plums with remaining glaze; turn steaks and plums and grill until steaks are browned on both sides and just lose their pink color throughout and plums are tender, about 3 minutes longer. Serve with rice, if desired.

Each serving: About 309 calories, 25g protein, 42g carbohydrate, 5g total fat (1g saturated), 66mg cholesterol, 524mg sodium.

Hoisin Honey-Glazed Pork Tenderloin with Grilled Pineapple

TOTAL TIME 30 minutes
MAKES 4 servings

1/4	cup hoisin sauce
1	tablespoon honey
1	tablespoon grated, peeled fresh ginger
1	teaspoon Asian sesame oil
1	pork tenderloin (1 1/4 pounds)
1/2	medium pineapple, untrimmed
2	tablespoons brown sugar

1. Prepare grill for covered direct grilling over medium heat.

2. In small bowl, with fork, stir hoisin, honey, ginger, and oil until blended.

3. Place pork on grill over medium heat; cover and grill pork, turning occasionally, 18 to 20 minutes.

4. Meanwhile, with serrated knife, cut pineapple half into 4 wedges; rub cut sides of pineapple with brown sugar.

5. Place pineapple on same grill rack with pork and grill, turning once, until browned on both sides, 10 minutes. While pineapple is grilling, brush pork with hoisin-honey glaze and turn frequently until meat on thermometer inserted in center of pork reaches 150°F. Transfer pork to cutting board; let stand 10 minutes. Temperature of pork will rise to 160°F upon standing. Transfer pineapple to platter.

6. Thinly slice pork and serve with pineapple wedges.

Each serving: About 275 calories, 31g protein, 23g carbohydrate, 6g total fat (2g saturated), 92mg cholesterol, 245mg sodium.

Available year-round, pineapples are picked ripe. Look for one that has crisp green leaves, is slightly soft to the touch and fragrant. Avoid any with dried, wilted, or yellow leaves or a strong, overly sweet aroma, which means that they have begun to ferment. Inspect the eyes to make sure they are free of mold. To check for ripeness, pull out a center leaf. It should release easily. This recipe calls for half a pineapple. Peel the remaining half, cut it into pieces, and store it in an airtight container in the refrigerator for up to four days. Use it with other tropical fruits for a light but tasty dessert.

This elegant dish pairs pork tenderloin medallions with a luscious cherry skillet sauce. An equal amount of dried cranberries can be substituted for the dried tart cherries, if you wish. Steamed rice with peas makes the perfect accompaniment.

Lucio's Pork Tenderloin

TOTAL TIME 25 minutes

MAKES 4 servings

    1   pork tenderloin (1¼ pounds), trimmed
  ¼   teaspoon salt
  ¾   cup water
  ¼   cup dried tart cherries
    1   teaspoon olive oil
    1   small onion, finely chopped
  ½   cup ruby port
  ½   teaspoon freshly grated orange peel

1. Cut pork tenderloin crosswise into 1¼-inch-thick rounds; press each with heel of hand to flatten slightly. Season with salt.
2. In microwave-safe cup or bowl, combine water and cherries; microwave on High 2 minutes. Let stand to allow cherries to plump.
3. Meanwhile, heat oil in nonstick 12-inch skillet over medium heat. Add pork in single layer. Sprinkle onion around pork; cook 4 minutes. Turn pork and stir onions; cook until pork is barely pink in center, about 4 minutes longer. With tongs, transfer pork to plate; cover loosely with foil to keep warm.
4. Add cherries with soaking liquid, port, and orange peel to skillet; heat to boiling. Boil until sauce is slightly syrupy, 1 to 2 minutes. Spoon cherry sauce over pork.

Each serving: About 230 calories, 34g protein, 12g carbohydrate, 5g total fat (1g saturated), 84mg cholesterol, 220mg sodium.

Gingered Pork and Vegetable Stir-fry

TOTAL TIME 30 minutes
MAKES 4 servings

1	pork tenderloin (12 ounces), trimmed and thinly sliced
2	tablespoons grated, peeled fresh ginger
1	cup reduced-sodium chicken broth
2	tablespoons teriyaki sauce
2	teaspoons cornstarch
2	teaspoons canola oil
8	ounces snow peas, strings removed
1	medium zucchini (8 ounces), cut lengthwise in half and thinly sliced crosswise
3	green onions, cut into 3-inch pieces

1. In medium bowl, toss pork and ginger. In cup, with fork, mix broth, teriyaki sauce, and cornstarch until smooth; set aside.

2. In nonstick 12-inch skillet, heat 1 teaspoon oil over medium heat until hot. Add snow peas, zucchini, and green onions and cook, stirring frequently (stir-frying), until lightly browned and tender-crisp, about 5 minutes. Transfer vegetables to large bowl.

3. In same skillet, heat remaining 1 teaspoon oil over medium heat until hot. Add pork mixture and stir-fry until pork just loses its pink color, about 3 minutes. Transfer pork to bowl with vegetables.

4. Stir cornstarch mixture; add to skillet and heat to boiling. Boil, stirring constantly, until sauce thickens slightly, about 1 minute. Return pork and vegetables to skillet and stir to coat with sauce; heat through.

Each serving: About 186 calories, 21g protein, 8g carbohydrate, 8g total fat (1g saturated), 55mg cholesterol, 430mg sodium.

When shopping for snow peas look for crisp, smooth, bright green pods. Stored in a zip-tight plastic bag, snow peas will keep in the refrigerator for up to four days, but they will lose some of their sweet flavor. If you want, buy extra to enjoy in another stir-fry later in the week. If snowpeas aren't available, use fresh sugar snap peas instead.

Orange Pork and Asparagus Stir-fry

TOTAL TIME 25 minutes

MAKE 4 servings

2	navel oranges
1	teaspoon olive oil
1	pork tenderloin (12 ounces), trimmed and thinly sliced on diagonal
$3/4$	teaspoon salt
$1/4$	teaspoon freshly ground black pepper
$1^1/2$	pounds thin asparagus, trimmed and cut in half
1	garlic clove, crushed with garlic press
$1/4$	cup water

The secret to a perfect orange pan sauce is simple: Be sure to wash and pat dry the orange first, and avoid the bitter white pith just below the peel when grating.

1. From 1 orange, grate 1 teaspoon peel and squeeze $1/4$ cup juice. Cut peel and white pith from remaining orange. Cut orange crosswise into $1/4$-inch-thick slices; cut each slice into quarters.

2. In nonstick 12-inch skillet, heat $1/2$ teaspoon oil over medium heat until hot but not smoking. Add half of pork slices and sprinkle with $1/4$ teaspoon salt and $1/8$ teaspoon pepper. Cook, stirring frequently (stir-frying), until pork just loses its pink color, about 2 minutes. With slotted spoon, transfer pork to plate. Repeat with remaining $1/2$ teaspoon oil, pork, $1/4$ teaspoon salt, and remaining $1/8$ teaspoon pepper.

3. To same skillet, add asparagus, garlic, orange peel, remaining $1/4$ teaspoon salt, and water; cover and cook, stirring occasionally, until asparagus is tender-crisp, about 2 minutes. Return pork to skillet. Add orange juice and orange pieces; heat through, stirring often.

Each serving: About 165 calories, 24g protein, 8g carbohydrate, 4g total fat (1g saturated), 50mg cholesterol, 495mg sodium.

Tarragon Pork Tenderloins with Grilled Grapes

TOTAL TIME 30 minutes

MAKES 8 servings

Want to grill like a pro? Invest in a pair of long-handled metal tongs. It makes turning larger pieces of meat, like whole pork tenderloins, a cinch. It also allows you to handle more delicate foods, like grilled grapes, with ease.

$^1/_2$ small shallot, cut in half
 3 tablespoons chopped fresh tarragon leaves
 2 tablespoons Dijon mustard
$^1/_2$ teaspoon salt
$^1/_2$ teaspoon freshly ground black pepper
 2 pork tenderloins (1 pound each)
 1 large bunch seedless red grapes (1$^1/_2$ pounds)
    lemon slices

1. Prepare grill for covered direct grilling over medium heat.

2. Meanwhile, press shallot through garlic press into cup; with fork, stir in tarragon, mustard, salt, and pepper. Smear tarragon mixture all over tenderloins.

3. Place tenderloins on grill; cover and grill, turning occasionally, until meat thermometer inserted in center of tenderloins reaches 150°F, 18 to 20 minutes. Internal temperature will rise to 160°F upon standing.

4. After tenderloins have cooked 15 minutes, add grapes to same grill rack with pork and grill, turning occasionally, until grapes soften slightly and brown in spots, 4 to 5 minutes.

5. Transfer tenderloins to cutting board. Let stand 5 minutes to set juices for easier slicing. Place grapes on large platter; with kitchen shears cut into eight clusters. To serve, thinly slice tenderloins and transfer to platter. Garnish with lemon slices.

Each serving: About 230 calories, 27g protein, 15g carbohydrate, 7g total fat (2g saturated), 78mg cholesterol, 215mg sodium.

Southern Peach Pork Chops

TOTAL TIME 25 minutes
MAKES 4 servings

This Bayou-inspired meal pairs spice-rubbed pork chops and juicy peaches both slathered with preserves before grilling. To prevent the food from sticking, be sure to give the grill rack a thin coat of oil before you fire it up. These luscious peaches also make a great summer dessert so add a few extra to the grill.

1 tablespoon curry powder
1 tablespoon brown sugar
1 tablespoon olive oil
1/2 teaspoon salt
1/4 teaspoon ground cinnamon
  pinch coarsely ground black pepper
1 garlic clove, crushed with garlic press
4 bone-in pork loin chops, 3/4 inch thick (5 ounces each)
4 large peaches, each cut in half and pitted
1/2 cup peach or apricot jam or preserves

1. Prepare grill for direct grilling over medium heat.

2. In cup, with fork, stir curry powder, sugar, oil, salt, cinnamon, pepper, and garlic until blended; use to rub on both sides of pork chops.

3. Brush cut side of each peach half and one side of chops with some jam. Place peaches, jam side down, and chops, jam side up, on grill over medium heat; grill 5 minutes. Turn chops and peaches; brush grilled side of chops with some jam and grill 5 minutes longer.

4. Transfer peaches as they are browned to platter. Turn chops and grill until browned on outside and still slightly pink inside, 2 to 3 minutes longer. Transfer chops to platter with peaches and serve.

Each serving: About 500 calories, 21g protein, 49g carbohy-drate, 26g total fat (9g saturated), 77mg cholesterol, 360mg sodium.

Pork Chops
with Cabbage and Pears

TOTAL TIME 25 minutes

MAKES 4 servings

2	teaspoons olive oil
4	bone-in pork loin chops, $1/2$ inch thick (6 ounces each)
$1^1/2$	teaspoons salt
$1/4$	teaspoon freshly ground black pepper
1	medium onion
2	ripe medium red or green Barlett pears, cored
1	cup apple cider
$1/2$	cup dry white wine
1	package (16 ounces) cabbage mix for coleslaw
2	teaspoons fresh thyme leaves

1. In nonstick 12-inch skillet, heat 1 teaspoon oil over medium heat until very hot. Add pork chops and sprinkle with $1/2$ teaspoon salt and $1/8$ teaspoon pepper; cook, turning chops once, until golden on outside and still slightly pink inside, and juices run clear when chop is pierced with tip of knife, about 7 minutes.

2. Meanwhile, thinly slice onion. Cut pears into $3/4$-inch wedges.

3. Transfer chops to plate; keep warm. Add remaining 1 teaspoon oil to skillet and cook onion, covered, until softened, about 5 minutes. Increase heat to medium-high. Add cider and wine; heat to boiling. Cook until sauce has thickened slightly, about 2 minutes.

4. Add pears, cabbage, thyme, remaining 1 teaspoon salt, and remaining $1/8$ teaspoon pepper and cook, covered, until pears and cabbage are tender, about 5 minutes. Return chops with any juice to skillet; heat through.

Each serving: About 375 calories, 25g protein, 31g carbohydrate, 17g total fat (5g saturated), 75mg cholesterol, 975mg sodium.

These days pork is almost as lean as white-meat chicken, but that's not a bad thing—it's healthier and more versatile than it once was. To boost its flavor, pork is often prepared with fruit, as in this recipe. To complete this skillet dinner, cider, cabbage and white wine are added. The result is a luscious main course with all the flavor and texture you could want. If desired, you can use two peeled and cored Golden Delicious apples instead of pears.

Chipotle Pork Chops with Corn Salad

TOTAL TIME **25 minutes**

MAKES **4 servings**

Chipotle pepper sauce is a made with dried chipotle peppers, which are smoked jalapeños. If you don't like smoky flavor, just substitute your favorite hot pepper sauce.

1	tablespoon chipotle pepper sauce
1	teaspoon ground cumin
1	teaspoon olive oil
1	garlic clove, crushed with garlic press
1/2	teaspoon salt
4	bone-in pork loin or rib chops, 3/4 inch thick (8 ounces each)
3	medium ears corn, husks and silk removed
2	medium tomatoes, chopped
1/2	avocado, pitted, peeled, and cut into 1/4-inch pieces
1/4	cup loosely packed cilantro leaves, chopped
2	tablespoons fresh lime juice

1. Prepare grill for covered direct grilling over medium heat.

2. In cup, with fork, stir chipotle sauce, cumin, oil, garlic, and 1/4 teaspoon salt. Use to rub on both sides of pork chops, coating them evenly.

3. Place pork chops on grill over medium heat; cover and grill, turning once, until pork chops are nicely browned on outside and still slightly pink inside, 10 to 11 minutes.

4. Meanwhile, cut kernels from corn and transfer to medium bowl. Add tomatoes, avocado, cilantro, lime juice, and remaining 1/4 teaspoon salt and stir to combine. Makes about 3 cups corn salad.

5. Serve corn salad with grilled pork chops and additional pepper sauce, if you like.

Each serving pork: About 455 calories, 35g protein, 1g carbohydrate, 32g total fat (11g saturated), 106mg cholesterol, 235mg sodium.

Each 1/4 cup corn salad: About 35 calories, 1g protein, 6g carbohydrate, 2g total fat (0g saturated), 0mg cholesterol, 55mg sodium.

Jerk Pork Chops with Grilled Pineapple

TOTAL TIME 25 minutes
MAKES 4 servings

- 2 garlic cloves, crushed with garlic press
- 1 tablespoon brown sugar
- 1 tablespoon vegetable oil
- 1 teaspoon dried thyme
- 1 teaspoon freshly grated lime peel
- 1 teaspoon ground allspice
- 1/2 teaspoon ground ginger
- 1/2 teaspoon salt
- 1/4 teaspoon ground red pepper (cayenne)
- 4 bone-in pork loin chops, 3/4 inch thick (8 ounces each), trimmed
- 1 ripe pineapple, trimmed, cored, with rind and eyes removed, and cut crosswise into 3/4-inch-thick slices
- 2 bunches green onions, trimmed
- 1 lime, cut into 4 wedges

Throwing a summer party? This spicy seasoning rub is also good with other cuts of pork, such as country-style or baby-back ribs, as well as with chicken wings and drumettes— perfect finger food to go with tropical drinks.

1. Prepare grill for covered direct grilling over medium heat.

2. In cup, with fork, stir garlic, sugar, oil, thyme, lime peel, allspice, ginger, salt, and ground red pepper; use to rub over pork chops.

3. Place chops on grill; cover and grill, turning once, until browned and still slightly pink in center, 12 to 15 minutes.

4. Meanwhile, place pineapple slices on same grill rack with chops and grill, turning once, until marks appear and flesh begins to char. Add whole green onions and grill, turning occasionally, 2 to 3 minutes.

5. Squeeze juice from lime wedges over pork. Serve pork chops with pineapple and green onions.

Each serving: About 440 calories, 39g protein, 26g carbohydrate, 21g total fat (6g saturated), 105mg cholesterol, 380mg sodium.

Pork Chops
with Tomato and Arugula

TOTAL TIME 20 minutes
MAKES 4 servings

For a fresh twist on pork chops, try these breaded and pan-fried chops served with peppery arugula and tomato salad on the side. If you want to extend the salad a little, add a small head of raddichio, torn, or serve with crusty French bread.

$1/3$	cup plain dried bread crumbs
$1/4$	cup freshly grated Romano cheese
1	teaspoon salt
1	large egg
4	boneless pork loin chops, $1/2$ inch thick (4 ounces each)
2	tablespoons olive oil
1	tablespoon fresh lemon juice
1	large ripe tomato (12 ounces)
$1/2$	small red onion
1	bag (4 to 5 ounces) baby arugula

1. On waxed paper, combine bread crumbs, Romano, and $1/2$ teaspoon salt. In pie plate, with fork, beat egg. Dip chops, one at a time, in egg, then in bread crumb mixture to coat. Repeat with remaining chops.

2. In nonstick 12-inch skillet, heat 1 tablespoon oil over medium-high heat. Add chops and cook, turning chops once, until juices run clear when chop is pierced with tip of knife, 5 to 6 minutes.

3. Meanwhile, in medium bowl, whisk lemon juice, remaining 1 tablespoon oil, and remaining $1/2$ teaspoon salt until blended. Coarsely chop tomato; thinly slice onion. Add arugula, onion, and tomato to bowl with dressing; toss until mixed and evenly coated with dressing.

4. Transfer chops to dinner plates; top with salad.

Each serving: About 370 calories, 31g protein, 14g carbohydrate, 22g total fat (6g saturated), 128mg cholesterol, 800mg sodium.

Pork Chops, Sausage Style

TOTAL TIME 25 minutes
MAKES 4 servings

1	tablespoon fennel seeds
1	garlic clove, crushed with garlic press
1	tablespoon olive oil
$3/4$	teaspoon salt
$3/4$	teaspoon coarsely ground black pepper
4	bone-in pork rib or loin chops, $3/4$ inch thick (6 ounces each)
2	red and/or yellow peppers, each cut into quarters
4	plum tomatoes, each cut lengthwise in half

1. Prepare grill for direct grilling over medium heat.

2. In mortar with pestle or in plastic bag with rolling pin, crush fennel seeds. In cup, with fork, mix fennel with garlic, oil, and $1/2$ teaspoon each salt and black pepper; use to rub on both sides of chops. Sprinkle cut sides of vegetables with remaining $1/4$ teaspoon each salt and pepper.

3. Arrange chops and peppers on grill over medium heat; cover and grill 5 minutes. Turn chops and peppers. Add tomatoes, cut sides down; cover and grill until chops are browned on outside and still slightly pink inside and vegetables are tender, 5 to 6 minutes.

Each serving: About 315 calories, 25g protein, 10g carbohydrate, 19g total fat (6g saturated), 70mg cholesterol, 490mg sodium.

Before these tasty chops hit the grill, they are seasoned with an olive oil–based rub of salt, pepper, garlic, and freshly crushed fennel seeds, a spice often used to flavor Italian sausage. You can substitute $3/4$ teaspoon ground fennel for the whole seeds, but freshly crushed seeds are far more flavorful.

Pork Chops
with Peppers and Onions

TOTAL TIME 30 minutes
MAKES 4 servings

Juicy pork loin chops are served on a bed of colorful sautéed red peppers and green onions. For even more vibrant color and flavor, substitute a yellow or orange pepper for one of the red peppers.

4	boneless pork loin chops, $1/2$ inch thick (4 ounces each), trimmed
$1/2$	teaspoon salt
$1/4$	teaspoon freshly ground black pepper
2	teaspoons olive oil
1	bunch green onions, green tops cut on diagonal into 3-inch pieces, white bottoms thinly sliced crosswise
2	medium red peppers, cut into $11/2$-inch pieces
1	garlic clove, crushed with garlic press
$1/8$	teaspoon crushed red pepper
$1/2$	cup chicken broth

1. Heat nonstick 12-inch skillet over medium heat until hot but not smoking. Add pork chops and sprinkle with salt and pepper. Cook, turning once, until lightly browned on outside and still slightly pink on inside, about 8 minutes. Transfer chops to plate; keep warm.

2. Add oil and green onion tops to skillet; cook 4 minutes. With slotted spoon, transfer green onion tops to small bowl.

3. In same skillet, add red peppers and green onion bottoms and cook, stirring occasionally, 8 minutes. Add garlic and crushed red pepper, and cook, stirring, 1 minute. Stir in broth and half of green onion tops; heat through.

4. To serve, transfer pepper mixture to platter; top with chops and remaining green onion tops.

Each serving: About 210 calories, 26g protein, 7g carbohydrate, 8g total fat (2g saturated), 71mg cholesterol, 495mg sodium.

Spiced Kielbasa and Summer Fruit Kabobs

(Pictured on page 2)

TOTAL TIME 20 minutes
MAKES 4 servings

Perfect fast summer-time fare, these sweet-and-spicy kabobs couldn't be easier to make. Just be sure that all the chunks to be skewered are the same size so that they make full contact with the grill. This way everything will cook evenly and finish at the same time. Serve on a bed of couscous or rice.

4   (10-inch) metal skewers
1   package (16 ounces) light kielbasa or other smoked sausages, cut crosswise into 1-inch-thick pieces
3   apricots, each pitted and cut into quarters
2   ripe plums or peaches, pitted and cut into 1-inch pieces
3   tablespoons sweet orange marmalade
1   teaspoon Chinese five-spice powder

1. Prepare grill for covered direct grilling over medium heat.

2. Meanwhile, alternately thread kielbasa, apricots, and plums onto skewers. In cup, with fork, stir marmalade and five-spice powder until blended.

3. Place skewers on grill over medium heat; cover and grill, turning occasionally, until kielbasa browns and fruit chars slightly, 5 minutes. Remove cover. Brush marmalade mixture all over kielbasa and fruit; grill, turning occasionally, 1 to 2 minutes longer.

Each serving: About 340 calories, 17g protein, 22g carbohydrate, 22g total fat (8g saturated), 76mg cholesterol, 1,032mg sodium.

CHAPTER 2

Poultry

Slow-Cooked Chicken Scarpariello

ACTIVE TIME 20 minutes SLOW-COOK 8 hours on Low or
4 hours on High MAKES 6 servings

We adapted this traditional Italian dish for the slow cooker. One secret to its extra-rich taste: coffee-colored cremini mushrooms (or baby portobellos), a variety of the common cultivated mushroom, which are actually more flavorful than their pale relations. You can keep fresh mushrooms wrapped in a damp cloth in the refrigerator for about one week.

8 ounces hot or sweet Italian sausage links, cut crosswise
    into $1^{1}/_{2}$-inch pieces
1 medium onion, chopped
2 garlic cloves, crushed with press
2 tablespoons tomato paste
2 tablespoons balsamic vinegar
1 teaspoon Italian seasoning or dried thyme
1 pint grape tomatoes
1 package (8 ounces) sliced cremini mushrooms
1 chicken ($3^{1}/_{2}$ to 4 pounds), cut into 8 pieces,
    skin removed from all but wings
$^{1}/_{4}$ teaspoon salt
$^{1}/_{4}$ teaspoon freshly ground black pepper

1. In 12-inch nonstick skillet, cook sausage pieces over medium heat, turning occasionally, until well browned, about 6 minutes. With tongs or slotted spoon, transfer sausages to 5- to 6-quart slow cooker. Add onion to skillet and cook until slightly softened, about 4 minutes. Stir in garlic and cook, stirring, 1 minute. Remove skillet from heat; stir in tomato paste, vinegar, and Italian seasoning until blended, then add tomatoes and mushrooms. Spoon vegetable mixture into slow cooker and stir to combine. Do not wash skillet.

2. Sprinkle chicken pieces with salt and pepper. In same skillet, cook chicken (in two batches, if necessary) over medium heat until well browned, about 10 minutes.

3. Place chicken pieces on top of vegetable mixture in slow cooker. Cover and cook as manufacturer directs, 8 hours on Low or 4 hours on High. Skim fat from juices before serving.

Each serving: About 355 calories, 39g protein, 9g carbohydrate, 17g total fat (6g saturated), 120mg cholesterol, 420mg sodium.

Creamy Chicken and Potatoes

ACTIVE TIME 20 minutes **SLOW-COOK** 8 hours on Low or 6 hours on High **MAKES** 6 servings

2   cups peeled baby carrots (from 16-ounce bag)
1   pound red potatoes, not peeled, cut into quarters
1   small onion, coarsely chopped
1   garlic clove, crushed with garlic press
1   chicken ($3^1/_2$ to 4 pounds), cut into 8 pieces and skin removed from all but wings
1   cup reduced-sodium chicken broth
3   tablespoons cornstarch
$^1/_2$ teaspoon dried thyme
1   teaspoon salt
$^1/_4$ teaspoon freshly ground black pepper
1   package (10 ounces) frozen peas, thawed
$^1/_2$ cup heavy or whipping cream

1. In 5- to 6-quart slow cooker, combine carrots, potatoes, onion, and garlic. Arrange chicken pieces on top of vegetables. In 2-cup liquid measuring cup, with fork, mix chicken broth, cornstarch, thyme, salt, and pepper; pour mixture over chicken and vegetables. Cover slow cooker with lid and cook as manufacturer directs, 8 hours on Low or 6 hours on High.

2. With slotted spoon, transfer chicken and vegetables to warm deep platter. Cover loosely with foil to keep warm.

3. Stir peas and cream into cooking liquid; heat through. To serve, spoon sauce over chicken and vegetables.

Each serving: About 380 calories, 36g protein, 30g carbohydrate, 12g total fat (6g saturated), 127mg cholesterol, 680mg sodium.

Attention chicken potpie lovers! Who says that you have to spend precious time and energy preparing a crust when what you really want is the filling? Here's a perfect family recipe. Along with a little help from the slow cooker, your meal will be ready exactly when you want it to be without your having to stand over the stove for hours.

Slow-Cooked Coq au Vin

ACTIVE TIME 20 minutes SLOW-COOK 8 hours on Low or
4 hours on High MAKES 4 servings

Our slow-cooker version of this French favorite is as flavorful as the original only more convenient. After browning the chicken, we sauté a *mirepoix*—French for mixture of chopped onion, carrot, and garlic—to season the sauce. *Mirepoix* can be used as seasoning for soups and stews or as a bed on which to braise meats or fish. You can also create your own *mirepoix* for your next roast chicken; it will deliver a very flavorful gravy.

3	slices bacon, each cut crosswise into $3/4$-inch pieces
1	package (10 ounces) mushrooms, cut in half
2	cups frozen pearl onions
1	chicken ($3^1/2$ to 4 pounds), cut into 8 pieces and skin removed from all but wings
$1/2$	teaspoon salt
$1/4$	teaspoon freshly ground black pepper
1	medium onion, chopped
1	large carrot, peeled and chopped
4	garlic cloves, chopped
1	cup dry red wine
2	tablespoons tomato paste
1	bay leaf
$3/4$	cup chicken broth

1. In 12-inch nonstick skillet, cook bacon over medium heat until browned. With slotted spoon, transfer bacon to paper towels to drain; set aside. Do not wash skillet.

2. Meanwhile, in 5- to 6-quart slow cooker, combine mushrooms and frozen pearl onions; set aside.

3. Sprinkle chicken pieces with salt and pepper. In skillet with drippings, cook chicken (in two batches, if necessary) over medium heat until evenly browned, about 10 minutes. Place chicken pieces on top of vegetables in slow cooker.

4. Discard drippings from skillet. Add onion and carrot and cook over medium heat, stirring frequently, until onion softens, 2 minutes. Stir in garlic and cook 1 minute. Add wine, tomato paste, and bay leaf; heat to boiling, stirring to dissolve tomato paste. Pour wine mixture and broth over chicken pieces. Cover slow cooker and cook as manufacturer directs, 8 hours on Low or 4 hours on High.

5. To serve, discard bay leaf. With large spoon, transfer chicken and sauce to deep platter; sprinkle with bacon.

Each serving: About 400 calories, 52g protein, 20g carbohydrate, 13g total fat (4g saturated), 156mg cholesterol, 690mg sodium.

Chicken Breasts à l'Orange

TOTAL TIME 25 minutes
MAKES 4 servings

1	package (6 ounces) quick-cooking white-and-wild rice mix
1	tablespoon butter or margarine
4	medium skinless, boneless chicken breast halves (1$^1/_4$ pounds)
$^1/_2$	teaspoon salt
2	medium oranges
$^1/_3$	cup sweet orange marmalade
2	tablespoons red wine vinegar
1	teaspoon cornstarch
1	small garlic clove, thinly sliced

1. Prepare rice mix as label directs.

2. Meanwhile, in nonstick 10-inch skillet, melt butter over medium heat. Add chicken breasts; sprinkle with $^1/_4$ teaspoon salt, and cook 5 minutes. Turn chicken and cook until juices run clear when thickest part of breast is pierced with tip of knife, 5 to 7 minutes longer. Transfer chicken to plate; keep warm. Do not wash skillet.

3. While chicken cooks, from 1 orange, grate $^1/_4$ teaspoon peel. Squeeze $^1/_2$ cup juice into 2-cup liquid measuring cup. Cut peel and white pith from second orange. Holding orange over same cup to catch juice, cut out sections from between membranes, allowing fruit to drop into cup. Squeeze juice from membranes. You should have at least $^3/_4$ cup orange juice and sections. With fork, stir in marmalade, vinegar, cornstarch, orange peel, and remaining $^1/_4$ teaspoon salt.

4. Add garlic to drippings in skillet; cook, stirring, 15 seconds. Add orange-juice mixture; heat to boiling. Boil until sauce thickens slightly, about 3 minutes. Return chicken with any juices to skillet; heat through, turning to coat with sauce. Serve with hot rice.

Each serving without rice: About 280 calories, 34g protein, 26g carbohydrate, 5g total fat (1g saturated), 82mg cholesterol, 435mg sodium.

Who knew that French cuisine could be this easy? Our speedy version of this bistro classic, uses skinless, boneless chicken breast halves instead of duck, and a quick fruity sauce, rather than a time-intensive complicated reduction. When juicing the oranges be sure to strain the pulp and seeds through a sieve.

Chicken and Prosciutto Roll-ups

TOTAL TIME **30 minutes**

MAKES **4 servings**

It's easy to stuff chicken breasts with creamy Fontina cheese. Just use a small, sharp knife and make about a 1-inch incision in the thickest part of the breast. The pocket will not be large, so you may have to fold the cheese slices in order to stuff them in.

- 4 medium skinless, boneless chicken breast halves (1$\frac{1}{4}$ pounds)
- 4 ounces Fontina cheese, cut into 4 slices
- 4 large slices prosciutto (2 to 2$\frac{1}{2}$ ounces)
- 12 large fresh basil leaves
  toothpicks
- 1 bag (6 ounces) prewashed baby spinach

1. Holding knife parallel to work surface, cut horizontal pocket in thickest part of each chicken breast. Stuff 1 cheese slice into each pocket.

2. Arrange prosciutto slices in single layer on work surface; top each with 3 basil leaves. Place 1 chicken breast half on each stack; wrap with prosciutto to cover pocket. Secure with toothpicks.

3. Heat nonstick 12-inch skillet over medium heat until hot. Add chicken; cover and cook 10 minutes. Remove cover; turn chicken and cook until it just loses its pink color throughout, 3 to 5 minutes longer. With slotted spoon, transfer chicken roll-ups to warm plate.

4. In same skillet, cook spinach, stirring constantly, until leaves wilt, about 1 minute.

5. To serve, remove toothpicks from chicken. Arrange spinach on dinner plates; top with chicken.

Each serving: About 295 calories, 44g protein, 2g carbohydrate, 12g total fat (6g saturated), 123mg cholesterol, 630mg sodium.

Skillet Chicken Parmesan

TOTAL TIME **20 minutes**

MAKES **4 servings**

1	teaspoon olive oil
1	pound thinly sliced chicken breast cutlets
1	container (15 ounces) refrigerated marinara sauce
4	ounces part-skim mozzarella cheese, shredded (1 cup)
2	plum tomatoes, chopped
2	tablespoons freshly grated Parmesan cheese
1	cup loosely packed fresh basil leaves, sliced

1. In nonstick 12-inch skillet, heat oil over medium heat until hot. Add half of chicken breasts to skillet and cook, turning once, until chicken just loses its pink color throughout, about 5 minutes. With tongs, transfer cooked chicken to plate; repeat with remaining chicken.

2. Return chicken breasts to skillet over medium heat; top with marinara sauce and mozzarella. Cover and cook until sauce is heated through and mozzarella has melted, 2 minutes. To serve, sprinkle with tomatoes, Parmesan, and basil.

Each serving: About 295 calories, 36g protein, 10g carbohydrate, 11g total fat (4g saturated), 84mg cholesterol, 660mg sodium.

Chicken stands in for the usual breaded, fried, and baked eggplant in this quick stovetop version of the Italian classic. For extra kick, try some bel paese or fontina in place of mozzarella.

Orange-Rosemary Skillet Chicken

TOTAL TIME 30 minutes
MAKES 4 servings

Leeks give this citrusy chicken a touch of sweetness, but if you want to skip washing them, substitute 1 medium chopped red onion.

4	medium skinless, boneless chicken breast halves (1$^1/_4$ pounds)
$^1/_2$	teaspoon salt
$^1/_8$	teaspoon freshly ground black pepper
1	tablespoon olive oil
2	medium leeks
2	oranges
$^1/_2$	cup reduced-sodium chicken broth
$^3/_4$	teaspoon chopped fresh rosemary

1. With meat mallet, or between two sheets of plastic wrap or waxed paper with rolling pin, pound chicken breast halves to even $^1/_2$-inch thickness; sprinkle with $^1/_4$ teaspoon salt and pepper.

2. In nonstick 12-inch skillet, heat oil over medium heat until hot. Add chicken breasts and cook, turning once, until browned on both sides and chicken loses its pink color throughout, 6 to 7 minutes. Transfer chicken to platter; cover loosely with foil to keep warm.

3. Meanwhile, cut off roots and trim dark green tops from leeks; cut each leek lengthwise in half, then crosswise into $^1/_4$-inch pieces. Rinse leeks in large bowl of cold water, swishing to remove sand. Transfer to colander to drain.

4. After removing chicken, add leeks to skillet; cover and cook over medium-low heat, stirring occasionally, until softened, 2 to 3 minutes.

5. Meanwhile, from 1 orange grate 1 teaspoon peel and squeeze $^1/_2$ cup juice. Halve and thinly slice remaining orange; set aside.

6. Add orange juice, chicken broth, rosemary, and juices from platter to skillet. Increase heat to medium-high and cook, stirring occasionally, until sauce is slightly reduced, about 3 minutes. Remove skillet from heat. Stir in reserved orange slices and peel and remaining $^1/_4$ teaspoon salt. Spoon sauce and oranges over chicken.

Each serving: About 245 calories, 34g protein, 14g carbohydrate, 5g total fat (1g saturated), 82mg cholesterol, 450mg sodium.

Chicken and Veggie Stir-fry

TOTAL TIME 22 minutes

MAKES 4 servings

1½	teaspoons olive oil
1	large yellow pepper, thinly sliced
2	cups shredded or matchstick carrots (from 10-ounce package)
4	small skinless, boneless chicken breast halves (1 pound), cut into ½-inch pieces
2	teaspoons finely chopped, peeled fresh ginger
2	garlic cloves, finely chopped
1	package (8.8 ounces) precooked brown rice
1	cup precooked shelled edamame (thawed, if frozen)
⅓	cup bottled stir-fry sauce
3	green onions, sliced

This delicious stir-fry is as pleasing to the eye as it is to the palate. If you can't find a yellow pepper, try a red, orange, or purple one. For even faster prep, use sliced pepper from the supermarket salad bar.

1. In nonstick 12-inch skillet, heat olive oil over medium heat until hot. Add yellow pepper and carrots and cook, stirring occasionally, 2 minutes. Add chicken pieces, ginger, and garlic, and cook, stirring frequently (stir-frying), 4 minutes.

2. Add brown rice, edamame, and stir-fry sauce, and cook, stirring occasionally, until chicken loses its pink color throughout and rice mixture is heated through, 2 to 3 minutes longer. Stir in green onions.

Each serving: About 375 calories, 38g protein, 37g carbohydrate, 8g total fat (1g saturated), 66mg cholesterol, 795mg sodium.

Thai-Style Coconut Chicken with Snow Peas

TOTAL TIME 30 minutes
MAKES 4 servings

Unsweetened coconut milk, a staple in Thai cuisine readily available at the supermarket, is a great ingredient to have handy if you're looking for rich, long-simmered flavor, but are pressed for time. If you can't find jasmine rice, substitute basmati or texmati, which is a cross between American long-grain rice and basmati.

1 cup jasmine rice or long-grain white rice
1 can (14 ounces) light coconut milk (not cream of coconut)
1 cup chicken broth
1 tablespoon cornstarch
4 thin slices peeled fresh ginger
2 strips (3" by $1/2$") fresh lime peel
1 pound skinless, boneless chicken breasts, cut into $1/2$-inch-wide strips
6 ounces snow peas (2 cups), strings removed
1 tablespoon reduced-sodium Asian fish sauce (nam pla or nuoc nam)
$1/4$ cup loosely packed fresh cilantro leaves, chopped lime wedges

1. Prepare rice as label directs.

2. Meanwhile, in 12-inch nonstick skillet, stir coconut milk, broth, cornstarch, ginger, and lime peel; heat to boiling over medium-high heat, stirring frequently. Boil 1 minute.

3. Add chicken and snow peas to skillet; cover and cook until chicken loses its pink color throughout, 4 to 5 minutes longer. Remove skillet from heat; stir in fish sauce and cilantro. Serve with rice and lime wedges.

Each serving: About 405 calories, 31g protein, 43g carbohydrate, 11g total (6g saturated), 66mg cholesterol, 465mg sodium.

Chicken Satay Lettuce Wraps

TOTAL TIME 20 minutes

MAKES 4 servings

These delicious chicken stuffed packets whipped up in a skillet with a silky peanut-butter sauce, is our speedy solution to traditional Asian grilled skewers. Use natural peanut butter if you prefer the filling to taste less sweet.

4	medium skinless, boneless chicken breast halves (1^1/4 pounds)
1	teaspoon curry powder
^{3}/4	teaspoon salt
2	limes
^{1}/4	cup creamy peanut butter
1	tablespoon soy sauce
1	teaspoon sugar
2	tablespoons very hot water
12	large green-leaf lettuce leaves
1	bunch fresh cilantro or mint
1	small cucumber, sliced

1. Grease 10-inch ridged grill pan or skillet with nonstick cooking spray. Heat over medium-high heat until very hot. Rub chicken breasts with curry powder and salt. Add chicken to skillet; cook, turning once, until it loses its pink color throughout, 10 to 12 minutes.

2. Meanwhile, from 1 lime, grate ^{1}/2 teaspoon peel and squeeze 1 tablespoon juice. Cut remaining lime into wedges.

3. In small serving bowl, with wire whisk, mix peanut butter, soy sauce, sugar, lime peel and juice, and water until sauce is blended and smooth.

4. With tongs, transfer cooked chicken to cutting board; cut into slices. Into each lettuce leaf, place 2 or 3 slices chicken, some cilantro sprigs, and some cucumber slices. Top each with sauce and fold over edges of lettuce to enclose. Serve with lime wedges.

Each serving: About 290 calories, 38g protein, 7g carbohydrate, 12g total fat (3g saturated), 91mg cholesterol, 850mg sodium.

Smoky Almond Chicken

TOTAL TIME 22 minutes
MAKES 4 servings

1/2 cup salted smoked almonds
1 slice firm white bread, torn into pieces
1/4 teaspoon freshly ground black pepper
1/4 cup reduced-fat sour cream
1/2 cup barbecue sauce (preferably less than
    260mg sodium per 2 tablespoons)
4 small skinless, boneless chicken breast halves (1 pound)

1. Preheat oven to 400°F. In food processor with knife blade attached, pulse almonds, bread, and pepper until coarsely chopped; transfer to waxed paper. In pie plate, mix sour cream with 1 tablespoon barbecue sauce until well blended.

2. Dip chicken breasts into sour-cream mixture, then roll in almond mixture, pressing to adhere mixture. Arrange chicken in single layer on ungreased cookie sheet. Bake until chicken loses its pink color throughout, 12 to 15 minutes. Serve with remaining sauce.

Each serving: About 311 calories, 32g protein, 12g carbohydrate, 15g total fat (2g saturated), 74mg cholesterol, 502mg sodium.

This sophisticated take on barbecue chicken starts with bottled sauce, but adds a crunchy coating of smoked almonds. You can also use whole natural almonds if you're seeking less smoky flavor.

Plum Balsamic Chicken

TOTAL TIME 30 minutes
MAKES 4 servings

4	medium skinless, boneless chicken breast halves (1^1/4 pounds)
^{1}/2	teaspoon salt
^{1}/8	teaspoon freshly ground black pepper
1	tablespoon olive oil
^{1}/2	medium red onion, chopped
3	small plums, each pitted and cut into 8 wedges
^{1}/2	cup reduced-sodium chicken broth
2	tablespoons balsamic vinegar
1	tablespoon honey

Chicken is the ideal foil for bold flavors—like this sweet-tangy combo of plums, balsamic vinegar, and honey. Select from a wide variety of black or purple plums, or try nectarines, for a tasty twist.

1. With meat mallet, or between two sheets of plastic wrap or waxed paper with rolling pin, pound chicken breast halves to ^{1}/2-inch thickness; sprinkle with ^{1}/4 teaspoon salt and pepper.

2. In nonstick 12-inch skillet, heat oil over medium heat until hot. Add chicken breasts and cook, turning once, until browned on both sides and chicken loses its pink color throughout, 6 to 7 minutes. Transfer chicken breasts to platter; cover loosely with foil to keep warm.

3. To same skillet, add onion and cook over medium heat, stirring frequently, until softened, 3 minutes. Add plums and cook, turning occasionally, until lightly browned, 3 minutes. Increase heat to medium-high. Stir in broth, balsamic vinegar, honey, remaining ^{1}/4 teaspoon salt, and any juices from platter; cook, stirring occasionally, until sauce is slightly reduced, 2 to 3 minutes. To serve, spoon sauce over chicken.

Each serving: About 240 calories, 34g protein, 13g carbohydrate, 6g total fat (1g saturated), 82mg cholesterol, 440mg sodium.

Apple-Dijon Chicken

TOTAL TIME 25 minutes

MAKES 4 servings

This autumn-inspired dish features maple syrup, which is used here to enhance the flavor of the apples and to provide a sweet counterpoint to the zesty Dijon mustard. For best results, look for 100% pure maple syrup, not "maple-flavored" syrup, which is a mixture of corn syrup and a very small amount of real maple syrup. Refrigerate syrup after opening.

4	medium skinless, boneless chicken breast halves (1^1/4 pounds)
^{1}/4	teaspoon salt
^{1}/8	teaspoon freshly ground black pepper
1	tablespoon olive oil
2	Golden Delicious apples, each cored and cut crosswise into 6 rings
1	small red onion, sliced
^{3}/4	cup reduced-sodium chicken broth
2	tablespoons maple syrup
1	tablespoon Dijon mustard with seeds
^{1}/3	cup half-and-half
1	teaspoon cornstarch

1. With meat mallet, or between two sheets of plastic wrap or waxed paper with rolling pin, pound chicken breast halves to even ^{1}/2-inch thickness; sprinkle with ^{1}/4 teaspoon salt and pepper.

2. In nonstick 12-inch skillet, heat oil over medium heat until hot. Add chicken breasts and cook, turning once, until browned on both sides and chicken loses its pink color throughout, 6 to 7 minutes. Transfer chicken breasts to platter; cover loosely with foil to keep warm. Do not wash skillet.

3. Meanwhile, in microwave-safe pie plate, combine apples and onion. Cover with waxed paper and microwave on High, stirring once, until tender, 3 to 4 minutes.

4. Add apple mixture to skillet and cook until browned, about 2 minutes. Add broth, maple syrup, mustard, and remaining ^{1}/4 teaspoon salt. Cook until broth mixture is slightly reduced, about 2 minutes.

5. In small bowl, blend half-and-half and cornstarch until smooth; stir into apple mixture with juices from platter. Cook until sauce is slightly thickened, about 1 minute. To serve, spoon sauce over chicken.

Each serving: About 295 calories, 34g protein, 21g carbohydrate, 8g total fat (2g saturated), 90mg cholesterol, 500mg sodium.

Green-Chile Skillet Chicken

TOTAL TIME 20 minutes
MAKES 4 servings

4	medium skinless, boneless chicken breast halves (1¼ pounds)
¼	teaspoon salt
⅛	teaspoon freshly ground black pepper
1	tablespoon olive oil
1	can (4 to 4½ ounces) diced green chiles, drained
1	cup grape tomatoes, each cut in half
¾	cup reduced-sodium chicken broth
½	teaspoon ground cumin
1	garlic clove, crushed with garlic press
2	tablespoons chopped fresh cilantro

This Tex-Mex specialty relies on canned green chiles for its heat—so shop for chopped chiles labeled mild, medium, or hot, depending on your preference.

1. With meat mallet, or between two sheets of plastic wrap or waxed paper with rolling pin, pound chicken breast halves to even ½-inch thickness; sprinkle with salt and pepper.

2. In nonstick 12-inch skillet, heat oil over medium heat until hot. Add chicken breasts and cook, turning once, until browned on both sides and chicken loses its pink color throughout, 6 to 7 minutes. Transfer chicken breasts to platter; cover loosely with foil to keep warm.

3. To skillet, add chiles, tomatoes, broth, cumin, garlic, and juices from platter; cook, stirring occasionally, until sauce is slightly reduced, about 3 minutes. Stir in cilantro. To serve, spoon sauce over chicken.

Each serving: About 205 calories, 33g protein, 4g carbohydrate, 5g total fat (1g saturated), 82mg cholesterol, 445mg sodium.

Mushroom-Marsala Skillet Chicken

TOTAL TIME 30 minutes

MAKES 4 servings

Marsala is a fortified wine from Sicily with a rich smoky flavor that ranges from dry to sweet. Dry marsala, sometimes served as an apéritif, is used in Italian cooking to flavor a number of popular dishes, such as this Chicken Marsala. Sweet marsala is used as a dessert wine as well as a flavoring for desserts such as zabaglione.

4 medium skinless, boneless chicken breast halves (1¹/₄ pounds)
¹/₂ teaspoon salt
¹/₈ teaspoon freshly ground black pepper
1 tablespoon olive oil
1 package (10 ounces) sliced cremini mushrooms
1 large shallot, finely chopped
¹/₂ cup reduced-sodium chicken broth
¹/₂ cup dry Marsala wine
2 tablespoons chopped fresh parsley

1. With meat mallet, or between two sheets of plastic wrap or waxed paper with rolling pin, pound chicken breast halves to even ¹/₂-inch thickness; sprinkle with ¹/₄ teaspoon salt and pepper.

2. In nonstick 12-inch skillet, heat oil over medium heat until hot. Add chicken breasts and cook, turning once, until browned on both sides and chicken loses its pink color throughout, 6 to 7 minutes. Transfer chicken breasts to platter; cover loosely with foil to keep warm.

3. To same skillet, add mushrooms, shallot, and remaining ¹/₄ teaspoon salt. Cook, stirring frequently, until mushrooms are browned, 3 minutes. Add broth, wine, and any juices from platter; cook, stirring occasionally, until sauce is reduced by half, about 4 minutes. Stir in parsley. To serve, spoon sauce over chicken.

Each serving: About 220 calories, 36g protein, 4g carbohydrate, 5g total fat (1g saturated), 82mg cholesterol, 470mg sodium.

Lemon-Mint Chicken Breasts on Watercress

TOTAL TIME 20 minutes

MAKES 4 servings

4	medium skinless, boneless chicken breast halves ($1^{1}/4$ pounds)
2	lemons
2	tablespoons olive oil
3	tablespoons chopped fresh mint
$^{1}/2$	teaspoon salt
$^{1}/4$	teaspoon coarsely ground black pepper
1	bag (4 ounces) baby watercress

1. Prepare grill for direct grilling over medium-high heat, or heat ridged grill pan over medium-high heat.

2. With meat mallet, or between two sheets of plastic wrap or waxed paper with rolling pin, pound chicken breast halves to even $^{1}/4$-inch thickness.

3. From lemons, grate 1 tablespoon plus $1^{1}/2$ teaspoons peel and squeeze 3 tablespoons juice. In large bowl, whisk lemon peel and juice, oil, 2 tablespoons mint, salt, and pepper until blended.

4. Reserve $^{1}/4$ cup dressing. In large bowl, toss chicken breasts with remaining dressing. Place chicken on grill over medium-high heat and grill, turning once, until juices run clear when breast is pierced with tip of knife, 4 to 5 minutes.

5. Meanwhile, in large bowl, toss watercress with reserved dressing. To serve, divide watercress among dinner plates and top each with chicken. Sprinkle with remaining chopped mint.

Each serving: About 225 calories, 34g protein, 2g carbohydrate, 9g total fat (1g saturated), 82mg cholesterol, 375mg sodium.

Fresh mint is often paired with lemon in Mediterranean cooking. Although dried herbs can often be substituted for fresh ones, we recommend that you use a fresh herb in this recipe. If mint isn't available, substitute fresh basil or Italian parsley.

Lime Chicken with Honeydew-Peach Salsa

TOTAL TIME 25 minutes

MAKES 4 servings

One of the most popular crossovers from Mexican cuisine, salsa has become a versatile accompaniment that can put the zing in even the blandest dish. The concept of salsa as a medley of chopped onion, tomatoes, chiles, cilantro, and other spices has expanded to include many different combinations, including a variety of fruits, like the one in this recipe.

1   lime
2   cups ($^{1}/_{4}$-inch pieces) honeydew melon ($^{1}/_{4}$ small melon)
1   large ripe peach, pitted and cut into $^{1}/_{4}$-inch pieces (2 cups)
$^{1}/_{2}$ cup loosely packed fresh basil leaves, coarsely chopped
$^{3}/_{4}$ teaspoon salt
4   medium skinless, boneless chicken breast halves ($1^{1}/_{4}$ pounds)
$^{1}/_{2}$ teaspoon coarsely ground black pepper

1. Prepare grill for covered direct grilling over medium heat.

2. From lime, grate $1^{1}/_{2}$ teaspoons peel and squeeze 2 tablespoons juice. In medium bowl, stir lime juice, melon, peach, basil, and $^{1}/_{4}$ teaspoon salt. Makes 4 cups salsa.

3. Place chicken breasts on plate. Sprinkle both sides with lime peel, remaining $^{1}/_{2}$ teaspoon salt, and pepper.

4. Place chicken on grill over medium-high heat; cover and grill, turning once, until juices run clear when thickest part of breast is pierced with tip of knife, 10 to 12 minutes. Transfer chicken to platter and serve with salsa.

Each serving: About 285 calories, 35g protein, 28g carbohydrate, 4g total fat (1g saturated), 90mg cholesterol, 525mg sodium.

Flame-Cooked Chicken Saltimbocca

TOTAL TIME 23 minutes

MAKES 8 servings

2	tablespoons fresh lemon juice
1	tablespoon olive oil
8	chicken cutlets or skinless, boneless chicken breast halves with tenderloins removed (2 pounds)
24	large fresh sage leaves
8	thin slices prosciutto (4 ounces)

1. Prepare grill for direct grilling over medium heat.

2. In large bowl, with fork, mix lemon juice and olive oil. Add chicken and toss to coat.

3. Place 3 sage leaves on each cutlet or breast half, then wrap each with 1 slice prosciutto. Place chicken on grill over medium heat and grill, turning once, until juices run clear when thickest part of breast is pierced with tip of knife, 8 minutes.

Each serving: About 195 calories, 31g protein, 1g carbohydrate, 7g total fat (2g saturated), 83mg cholesterol, 410mg sodium.

Wrapping delicate chicken breasts in prosciutto before grilling keeps them nice and juicy. Italian prosciutto, a seasoned, salt-cured (but not smoked), air-dried ham imparts rich flavor to the dish. If you can't find it, substitute slices of lean bacon or Canadian bacon.

Double-Dipped Potato-Chip Chicken with Quick Slaw

TOTAL TIME 30 minutes
MAKES 4 servings

The potato-chip coating on the chicken and the cabbage-and-carrot slaw earn this dish an A+ for crunch and texture. You can also substitute the preshredded broccoli "slaw" that's usually found packaged in your supermarket's refrigerated produce case.

1¼ cups crushed potato chips
1 large egg
4 medium skinless, boneless chicken breast halves (1¼ pounds)
¼ teaspoon plus ⅛ teaspoon freshly ground black pepper
4 cups (from 16-ounce bag) shredded cabbage mix for coleslaw
1 large carrot, peeled and shredded
¼ small red onion, thinly sliced
¼ cup cider vinegar
1 tablespoon vegetable oil
1 teaspoon sugar
½ teaspoon salt
¼ cup light mayonnaise
2 tablespoons barbecue sauce

1. Preheat oven to 450°F.

2. Place crushed chips on large plate. With fork, beat egg in pie plate or shallow dish. Dip 1 chicken breast half in egg, then transfer to crumbs in plate, pressing chicken so crumbs adhere. Transfer chicken to ungreased cookie sheet. Repeat with remaining chicken.

3. Dip chicken again in remaining crumbs so that chicken is completely coated. Return chicken to cookie sheet. Sprinkle both sides of chicken with ¼ teaspoon pepper. Bake just until chicken loses its pink color throughout, about 15 minutes.

4. Meanwhile, in large bowl, toss cabbage mix with carrot, onion, vinegar, oil, sugar, salt, and remaining ⅛ teaspoon pepper until well combined. In small bowl, stir mayonnaise and barbecue sauce until well blended.

5. To serve, spoon barbecue mayonnaise into 4 small cups. Divide chicken and slaw among 4 dinner plates and serve with mayonnaise.

Each serving: About 460 calories, 38g protein, 30g carbohydrate, 21g total fat (4g saturated), 140mg cholesterol, 755mg sodium.

Chicken Grilled in Foil Packet

ACTIVE TIME 15 minutes TOTAL TIME 30 minutes
MAKES 4 servings

Known in France as *en papillote*, this technique is designed to keep delicate foods from drying out during cooking and to enhance the aroma of the dish. Traditionally, the bags are opened at the table, so diners can savor the fragrance. You can find foil cooking bags in most supermarkets, but, if not, you can make your own: Layer two 24" by 18" sheets of heavy-duty foil. Place the ingredients in the center. Bring the short ends of the foil up and over the ingredients and fold them over two or three times to seal tightly. Fold over the remaining sides of foil two or three times to completely seal in the juices.

4 medium skinless, boneless chicken breast halves
    (1^1/4 pounds)
3 tablespoons drained capers, chopped
2 tablespoons butter or margarine, cut into pieces
^{1}/4 teaspoon coarsely ground black pepper
^{1}/4 cup loosely packed fresh parsley leaves, chopped
2 teaspoons cornstarch
1 tablespoon water

1. Prepare grill for direct grilling over medium heat.

2. Place chicken breast halves, capers, butter, pepper, and 2 tablespoons parsley in 17" by 15" extra-heavy-duty foil cooking bag. In cup, blend cornstarch and water until smooth. Add cornstarch mixture to bag and fold to seal as label directs. Shake bag gently to combine ingredients.

3. Place foil packet on grill over medium heat and cook chicken, turning packet once halfway through cooking, 15 minutes. Remove packet from grill; let stand 5 minutes.

4. Before serving, with kitchen shears, cut an X in top of foil packet to allow steam to escape. Open packet and check to make sure that juices run clear when thickest part of chicken breast is pierced with tip of knife. Sprinkle chicken with remaining 2 tablespoons parsley and serve.

Each serving: About 215 calories, 33g protein, 2g carbohydrate, 8g total fat (5g saturated), 98mg cholesterol, 342mg sodium.

Mushroom and Marsala Chicken

Prepare chicken as directed, but omit capers in Step 2 and add **8 ounces sliced mushrooms, 2 tablespoons dry or sweet Marsala wine, $1/2$ teaspoon salt,** and **1 garlic clove,** crushed with garlic press, to packet before grilling. In Step 4, sprinkle with an additional **1 tablespoon Marsala wine** before serving.

Each serving: About 230 calories, 34g protein, 4g carbohydrate, 8g total fat (5g saturated), 98mg cholesterol, 632mg sodium.

Buffalo-Style Chicken

Prepare chicken as directed, but omit capers in Step 2 and add **3 tablespoons cayenne pepper sauce** to packet before grilling. Serve chicken with **3 medium carrots,** peeled and cut into 3-inch-long sticks, **3 celery stalks,** cut into 3-inch-long sticks, and **1 ounce crumbled blue cheese** ($1/4$ cup).

Each serving: About 265 calories, 35g protein, 8g carbohydrate, 10g total fat (6g saturated), 104mg cholesterol, 882mg sodium.

Grilled Chicken Breasts with Tomato-Olive Relish

TOTAL TIME 25 minutes

MAKES 4 servings

Look for pitted Kalamata olives in the deli section of the supermarket. You can also substitute Gaeta or even Spanish green olives.

2 ripe medium tomatoes, each chopped into $1/4$-inch pieces

$1/4$ cup plus 1 tablespoon pitted and coarsely chopped Kalamata olives

2 tablespoons finely chopped red onion

2 tablespoons capers, drained

1 teaspoon red wine vinegar

3 teaspoons olive oil

4 small skinless, boneless chicken breast halves (1 pound)

$1/4$ teaspoon salt

$1/4$ teaspoon coarsely ground black pepper

1. In small bowl, toss tomatoes, $1/4$ cup olives, onion, capers, vinegar, and 1 teaspoon olive oil; set aside.

2. Prepare grill for direct grilling over medium heat.

3. In medium bowl, toss chicken breasts with salt, pepper, and remaining 2 teaspoons oil until evenly coated.

4. Place chicken on grill over medium heat and grill, turning once, until juices run clear when thickest part of chicken is pierced with tip of knife, 5 to 6 minutes per side.

5. To serve, top chicken with tomato-olive relish and sprinkle with remaining 1 tablespoon olives.

Each serving: About 200 calories, 27g protein, 5g carbohydrate, 7g total fat (1g saturated), 66mg cholesterol, 565mg sodium.

Chicken Tenders Picadillo

TOTAL TIME 30 minutes
MAKES 4 servings

1	tablespoon olive oil
1	pound chicken breast tenders, thinly sliced
1	medium onion, chopped
1	garlic clove, crushed with garlic press
1/2	teaspoon ground cumin
1	cup salsa
1/4	cup raisins
1/2	cup salad olives or pimiento-stuffed green olives, chopped
4	burrito-size flour tortillas

An important flavoring in Middle Eastern, Asian, and Latin-American cuisine, cumin is prized for its aroma and nutty flavor. Here we use ground cumin to flavor our stream-lined version of a traditional Latino favorite. If you only have the seeds, you can grind them in a spice grinder or place the seeds between two sheets of waxed paper and finely crush them with a heavy-bottomed pan or rolling pin.

1. In 12-inch nonstick skillet, heat oil over medium heat until hot. Add chicken and cook, turning once, until golden, 4 to 6 minutes. With slotted spoon, transfer chicken to bowl.

2. Add onion to skillet and cook over medium heat until lightly browned, 6 to 8 minutes. Stir in garlic and cumin; cook 1 minute. Stir in salsa, raisins, olives, and chicken; heat to boiling over medium-high heat.

3. Meanwhile, wrap flour tortillas in damp paper towels and microwave on High 1 minute. Serve picadillo with warm tortillas.

Each serving: About 450 calories, 33g protein, 51g carbohydrate, 13g total fat (3g saturated), 66mg cholesterol, 1,205mg sodium.

Oven-Fried Chicken Tenders with Five-Spice BBQ Sauce

TOTAL TIME 30 minutes
MAKES 4 servings

3/4	cup panko (Japanese-style bread crumbs)
2	tablespoons sesame seeds
1	large egg white
1	teaspoon Chinese five-spice powder
1/2	teaspoon salt
1	pound chicken breast tenders
1	tablespoon olive oil
1	small onion, chopped
1/2	cup ketchup
1	tablespoon brown sugar
1 1/2	teaspoons cider vinegar
1 1/2	teaspoons Worcestershire sauce

Chinese five-spice powder, a robust blend of cinnamon, cloves, fennel seed, star anise, and Szechuan peppercorns is a handy helper when you want to keep the number of ingredients to a minimum. It is available in Asian markets and most supermarkets.

1. Preheat oven to 475°F. In 10-inch skillet, toast bread crumbs and sesame seeds over high heat, stirring frequently, until golden, about 5 minutes. Transfer crumb mixture to plate. Do not wash skillet.

2. In medium bowl, with wire whisk or fork, mix egg white, 1/2 teaspoon five-spice powder, and salt until foamy. Dip chicken tenders in egg-white mixture, then in crumb mixture to coat. Place tenders on cookie sheet. Bake tenders, without turning, until they lose their pink color throughout, 13 to 15 minutes.

3. Meanwhile, in same skillet, heat oil over medium heat until hot. Add onion and cook until soft and lightly browned, 8 to 10 minutes. Remove skillet from heat; stir in ketchup, brown sugar, vinegar, Worcestershire, and remaining 1/2 teaspoon five-spice powder. Pour sauce into small bowl and serve with tenders.

Each serving: About 280 calories, 30g protein, 23g carbohydrate, 8g total fat (1g saturated), 66mg cholesterol, 775mg sodium.

Speedy Paella

TOTAL TIME 30 minutes

MAKES 4 servings

The unofficial national dish of Spain, paella is usually very time-intensive to make, but thanks to chicken tenders and seasoned rice mix we've sped up the process so that you can have it on the table in a mere thirty minutes.

 1 package (3$^{1}/_{2}$ ounces) fully cooked chorizo or pepperoni, cut crosswise into $^{1}/_{4}$-inch-thick pieces
 1 pound chicken breast tenders, cut crosswise into thirds
 1 medium red pepper, chopped
 1 garlic clove, crushed with garlic press
 $^{1}/_{8}$ teaspoon dried thyme
 1 package (8 ounces) Spanish-style yellow-rice mix
 2 cups water
 1 package (10 ounces) frozen peas

1. In nonstick 12-inch skillet, cook chorizo over medium heat, stirring occasionally, until fat is rendered, 2 to 3 minutes. With slotted spoon, transfer chorizo to plate.

2. To same skillet, add chicken tenders and cook until they lose their pink color throughout, 3 to 4 minutes; with slotted spoon, transfer chicken to plate.

3. To same skillet, add red pepper, garlic, and thyme and cook, stirring, 1 minute. Add rice mix, water, and chorizo; heat to boiling over medium-high heat. Reduce heat to medium-low; cover and cook 10 minutes.

4. Stir frozen peas into rice mixture and cook, covered, 5 minutes. Stir in chicken and heat through. Serve hot.

Each serving: About 490 calories, 42g protein, 54g carbohydrate, 12g total fat (4g saturated), 88mg cholesterol, 1,455mg sodium.

Sesame Thighs
with Hoisin Dipping Sauce

TOTAL TIME 30 minutes
MAKES 4 servings

8	small bone-in chicken thighs (2 pounds), skin and fat removed
$1/4$	cup plus 2 tablespoons hoisin sauce
2	tablespoons sesame seeds
2	tablespoons chili sauce
$1^1/2$	teaspoons chopped, peeled fresh ginger
$1^1/2$	teaspoons rice vinegar
$1/4$	teaspoon Chinese five-spice powder

Good idea: When removing the chicken skin, you'll get a good grip with less mess by holding the skin with a paper towel while peeling it away from the meat.

1. Preheat oven to 475°F.

2. Arrange chicken thighs in $15^1/2$" by $10^1/2$" jelly-roll pan. Into cup, pour $1/4$ cup hoisin sauce; use to brush both sides of thighs. Sprinkle with sesame seeds. Bake until juices run clear when thickest part of thigh is pierced with knife, 20 to 25 minutes.

3. Meanwhile, prepare dipping sauce: In microwave-safe cup, combine chili sauce, ginger, vinegar, five-spice powder, and remaining 2 tablespoons hoisin sauce. Just before serving, heat mixture in microwave oven on High 45 seconds, stirring once. Serve chicken with dipping sauce.

Each serving: About 305 calories, 29g protein, 14g carbohydrate, 14g total fat (4g saturated), 100mg cholesterol, 535mg sodium.

Pan-Seared Chicken Thighs with Warm Pear and Celery Slaw

TOTAL TIME **20 minutes**
MAKES **4 servings**

To turn these Bartlett pears into even, match-stick-thin strips effortlessly and quickly, a great tool to use is an inexpensive mandoline or V-slicer. It also makes scalloped potatoes and cole slaw.

1	teaspoon olive oil
1	pound skinless, boneless chicken thighs, cut into 1-inch-wide strips
$1/2$	teaspoon salt
$1/4$	teaspoon freshly ground black pepper
2	medium Bartlett pears, not peeled
2	stalks celery
2	tablespoons lemon juice
1	shallot, finely chopped
$3/4$	cup apple cider
1	tablespoon Dijon mustard
1	tablespoon chopped fresh parsley leaves

1. In 12-inch nonstick skillet, heat oil over medium heat until hot. Add chicken thighs to skillet and sprinkle with salt and pepper. Cook thighs, turning once, until they lose their pink color throughout, 8 to 10 minutes. With tongs, transfer chicken to warm plate. Do not wash skillet.

2. Meanwhile, cut each pear lengthwise in half; discard core. Cut halves lengthwise into $1/2$-inch matchstick strips. Thinly slice celery on diagonal. In large bowl, toss pear and celery slices with lemon juice; set aside.

3. To same skillet, add shallot and cook, stirring constantly, until it begins to brown, 30 seconds to 1 minute. Add cider and heat to boiling over high heat; whisk in mustard. Pour cider dressing over pear mixture and toss to coat. Sprinkle chicken thighs with parsley and serve with slaw.

Each serving: About 230 calories, 23g protein, 21g carbohydrate, 6g total fat (1g saturated), 94mg cholesterol, 430mg sodium.

Slow-Cooker Latin Chicken with Black Beans and Sweet Potatoes

ACTIVE TIME 20 minutes **SLOW-COOK** 8 hours on Low or 4 hours on High **MAKES** 6 servings

3	pounds bone-in chicken thighs, skin and fat removed
2	teaspoons ground cumin
1/4	teaspoon salt
1/4	teaspoon freshly ground black pepper
1	teaspoon smoked paprika or 1/2 teaspoon chopped chipotle chiles in adobo sauce
1/2	teaspoon ground allspice
1	cup reduced-sodium chicken broth
1/2	cup salsa
3	large garlic cloves, crushed with garlic press
2	cans (15 to 19 ounces each) black beans, rinsed and drained
2	pounds sweet potatoes, peeled and cut into 2-inch pieces
1	roasted red pepper from jar, cut into strips (1 cup)
1/3	cup loosely packed fresh cilantro leaves, chopped
	lime wedges

1. Sprinkle chicken thighs with 1/2 teaspoon ground cumin, salt, and pepper. Heat 12-inch nonstick skillet over medium heat until hot. Add chicken thighs and cook until well browned on all sides, about 10 minutes. With tongs, transfer chicken to plate. Remove skillet from heat.

2. In same skillet, combine smoked paprika, allspice, broth, salsa, garlic, and remaining 1 1/2 teaspoons cumin.

3. In 6-quart slow cooker, combine beans and sweet potatoes. Arrange chicken thighs in single layer on top of potato mixture; pour broth mixture over chicken. Cover slow cooker and cook as manufacturer directs, 8 hours on Low or 4 hours on High.

4. With tongs or slotted spoon, transfer chicken thighs to large platter. Gently stir roasted red pepper strips into potato mixture; spoon mixture over chicken. Sprinkle with cilantro and serve with lime wedges.

Each serving: About 415 calories, 36g protein, 61g carbohydrate, 6g total fat (1g saturated), 107mg cholesterol, 875mg sodium.

Paprika, made from finely ground, dried red peppers, is available in three basic types: sweet, half-sweet, and hot. Those from Spain and Hungary are considered to be the most flavorful. Smoked paprika is highly prized for its pungent yet mellow flavor. Look for smoked paprika in gourmet or spice shops, or use Hungarian hot paprika, which you can find in most supermarkets.

Slow-Cooker Chicken Tagine

ACTIVE TIME 20 minutes SLOW-COOK 8 hours on Low or
4 hours on High MAKES 6 servings

The best way to peel butternut squash is to cut it into smaller pieces first: Holding it firmly on its side and using a sharp knife, cut it crosswise into 2-inch-thick rounds. Place each round, flat side down, and cut away the peel. Then scoop out the seeds and cut as desired. If you want to save time and effort, however, you can opt for a package of peeled, precut butternut squash that is available in the produce section of many supermarkets.

- 1 medium butternut squash (1 1/2 pounds), peeled and cut into 2-inch pieces
- 2 medium tomatoes, coarsely chopped
- 1 medium onion, chopped
- 2 garlic cloves, crushed with garlic press
- 1 can (15 to 19 ounces) garbanzo beans, rinsed and drained
- 1 cup reduced-sodium chicken broth
- 1/3 cup raisins
- 2 teaspoons ground coriander
- 2 teaspoons ground cumin
- 1/2 teaspoon ground cinnamon
- 1/2 teaspoon salt
- 1/4 teaspoon freshly ground black pepper
- 3 pounds bone-in chicken thighs, skin and fat removed
- 1 box (10 ounces) plain couscous
- 1/2 cup pitted green olives

1. In 6-quart slow cooker, combine squash, tomatoes, onion, garlic, beans, broth, and raisins. In cup, combine coriander, cumin, cinnamon, salt, and pepper. Rub spice mixture over chicken thighs. Arrange chicken thighs on top of vegetable mixture. Cover slow cooker and cook as manufacturer directs, 8 hours on Low or 4 hours on High.

2. About 10 minutes before serving, prepare couscous as label directs. Fluff with fork.

3. Gently stir olives into tangine. Serve over couscous.

Each serving: About 545 calories, 39g protein, 80g carbohydrate, 9g total fat (2g saturated), 107mg cholesterol, 855mg sodium.

Red-Cooked Chicken with Stir-fry Vegetables, Slow Cooker–Style

ACTIVE TIME 20 minutes SLOW-COOK 8 hours on Low or 4 hours on High MAKES 4 servings

Traditional Chinese "red cooked" chicken involves slowly cooking it in a soy sauce–based liquid which gives the dish a deep red color. We employ the same method here, only using the convenience of the slow cooker.

$1/2$ cup dry sherry
$1/3$ cup soy sauce
$1/4$ cup packed brown sugar
2 tablespoons grated, peeled fresh ginger
1 teaspoon Chinese five-spice powder
3 garlic cloves, crushed with garlic press
1 bunch green onions, cut into 2-inch pieces (white and green parts separated)
3 pounds bone-in chicken thighs, skin and fat removed
1 bag (16 ounces) fresh vegetables for stir-fry (such as snow peas, carrots, broccoli, red pepper)

1. In 5- to 6-quart slow cooker, combine sherry, soy sauce, sugar, ginger, five-spice powder, garlic, and white parts of green onions. (Coarsely chop remaining green parts; wrap and refrigerate until serving time.) Add chicken thighs and toss to coat with sherry mixture. Cover slow cooker and cook as manufacturer directs, 8 hours on Low or 4 hours on High.
2. Just before serving, place vegetables in microwave-safe medium bowl and cook in microwave as label directs.
3. With tongs, transfer chicken thighs to deep platter. Stir vegetables into sauce in slow cooker. Spoon vegetable mixture around chicken. Sprinkle with green onions.

Each serving: About 355 calories, 43g protein, 27g carbohydrate, 8g total fat (2g saturated), 161mg cholesterol, 1,515mg sodium.

Chicken and Basil Stir-fry

TOTAL TIME 30 minutes

MAKES 4 servings

1 lime
1 pound skinless, boneless chicken thighs, cut into 1-inch chunks
1 tablespoon low-sodium soy sauce
1 teaspoon canola oil
1 bag (12 ounces) trimmed green beans, cut in half
2 tablespoons water
2 garlic cloves, thinly sliced
1 cup loosely packed fresh basil leaves, sliced
1 tablespoon reduced-sodium Asian fish sauce (nam pla or nuoc nam)
  cooked jasmine rice (optional)

Fresh basil gives this Asian specialty its rich aromatic flavor. You can also substitute an equal amount of whole cilantro leaves.

1. From lime, grate 1 teaspoon peel and squeeze 1 tablespoon juice. In medium bowl, toss chicken with lime peel and soy sauce; set aside.

2. In nonstick 12-inch skillet, heat oil over medium heat until hot. Add beans and water; cook, stirring often, 4 minutes. Add garlic and cook until beans are tender-crisp, about 2 minutes. With slotted spoon, transfer bean mixture to bowl.

3. In same skillet, cook chicken mixture over medium heat, stirring frequently (stir-frying), until chicken loses its pink color throughout, about 5 minutes. Remove skillet from heat; stir in bean mixture, basil, fish sauce, and lime juice. Serve with rice, if you like.

Each serving without rice: About 185 calories, 25g protein, 9g carbohydrate, 6g total fat (1g saturated), 94mg cholesterol, 460mg sodium.

Chicken Stir-fry with Cabbage

TOTAL TIME 30 minutes
MAKES 4 servings

1	cup long-grain white rice
1	tablespoon vegetable oil
1	garlic clove, crushed with garlic press
1	pound skinless, boneless chicken thighs, cut into 1-inch pieces
3	green onions, cut into $1\frac{1}{2}$-inch pieces
1	medium red pepper, thinly sliced
$\frac{1}{2}$	small head green cabbage, cut into 1-inch pieces (about 4 cups)
1	cup reduced-sodium chicken broth
2	tablespoons reduced-sodium soy sauce
1	tablespoon cornstarch
2	teaspoons grated, peeled fresh ginger

1. Prepare rice as label directs.

2. Meanwhile, in 12-inch nonstick skillet, heat oil and garlic over medium heat until hot. Add chicken and green onions and cook, stirring frequently (stir-frying), until chicken is well browned and loses its pink color throughout, 5 to 6 minutes. With slotted spoon, transfer mixture to medium bowl.

3. To same skillet, add red pepper, cabbage, and $\frac{1}{4}$ cup broth; stir to combine. Cover and cook over medium heat, stirring occasionally, until vegetables are tender-crisp, about 5 minutes. Transfer vegetables to bowl with chicken.

4. Meanwhile, in cup, stir soy sauce, cornstarch, ginger, and remaining $\frac{3}{4}$ cup broth until blended and smooth. Add broth mixture to skillet and heat to boiling over high heat; boil 1 minute. Remove skillet from heat. Stir chicken and vegetables into broth mixture; heat through. Serve with rice.

Each serving: About 385 calories, 29g protein, 48g carbohydrate, 9g total fat (2g saturated), 94mg cholesterol, 525mg sodium.

Preparing the cabbage for this crunchy stir-fry is really a snap. All you do is cut the head in half (or in fourths, if using a large head) and, holding the top of each piece firmly, slice the core from the center to the base or cut around the core from the base. After removing and discarding the core, place each piece cut side down and cut into pieces of the desired size. Wrap the unused portion tightly in plastic wrap and refrigerate. Use within two days.

Deviled Chicken Thighs with Mashed Sweet Potatoes

TOTAL TIME 30 minutes

MAKES 4 servings

This recipe calls for coating the chicken with panko, Japanese-style crumbs. These delicate crystal-shaped crumbs create a lighter and crunchier crust than traditional dried bread crumbs. You can find them in Asian food markets and in the Asian food section of some supermarkets. Store them in a rigid plastic container with a tightly fitting lid or in a zip-tight plastic bag in the refrigerator for up to one month.

1/4 cup Dijon mustard
2 tablespoons Worcestershire sauce
1/4 teaspoon ground red pepper (cayenne)
1 garlic clove, crushed with garlic press
1/3 cup panko (Japanese-style bread crumbs)
1/4 cup loosely packed fresh parsley leaves, chopped
2 pounds skinless, boneless chicken thighs, cut into 1-inch-wide strips
4 medium sweet potatoes (12 ounces each), not peeled
1 tablespoon butter or margarine
1/4 teaspoon salt
1/4 teaspoon freshly ground black pepper

1. Preheat broiler. Grease 15 1/2" by 10" jelly-roll pan or broiler pan.

2. In large bowl, stir mustard, Worcestershire, ground red pepper, and garlic until blended. On waxed paper, combine bread crumbs and parsley.

3. Toss chicken with mustard mixture until evenly coated. Arrange chicken in single layer in jelly-roll pan. Place pan in broiler 5 to 7 inches from heat source and broil 8 minutes. Remove pan from broiler; sprinkle chicken with crumbs (do not turn chicken). Return pan to broiler and broil until crumbs are browned and juices run clear when thickest part of thigh is pierced with knife, about 2 minutes longer.

4. Meanwhile, place whole potatoes in microwave-safe large bowl; cover with vented plastic wrap. Microwave potatoes on High 5 minutes. Rearrange potatoes and cook until tender, about 5 minutes longer. Cool potatoes 5 minutes. Cut each potato lengthwise in half and scoop flesh from skin into same bowl; discard skin. Add butter, salt, and pepper. With potato masher, coarsely mash potatoes. Serve chicken with sweet potatoes.

Each serving: About 581 calories, 46g protein, 52g carbohydrate, 20g total fat (7g saturated), 156mg cholesterol, 837mg sodium.

Summer Squash and Chicken

TOTAL TIME 30 minutes
MAKES 4 servings

1	lemon
1	tablespoon olive oil
$1/2$	teaspoon salt
$1/4$	teaspoon coarsely ground black pepper
4	skinless, boneless chicken thighs ($1^1/4$ pounds)
4	medium yellow summer squashes and/or zucchini (8 ounces each), each cut lengthwise into 4 wedges
$1/4$	cup snipped fresh chives

1. From lemon, grate 1 tablespoon peel and squeeze 3 tablespoons juice. In medium bowl, with wire whisk, mix lemon peel and juice, oil, salt, and pepper; transfer 2 tablespoons to cup.

2. Add chicken thighs to bowl with lemon marinade; cover and let stand 10 minutes at room temperature or 30 minutes in the refrigerator.

3. Meanwhile, prepare grill for covered direct grilling over medium heat.

4. Discard marinade. Place chicken thighs and squash on grill over medium heat; cover and grill, turning chicken and squash once and removing pieces as they are done, until chicken loses its pink color throughout and squash is tender and browned, 10 to 12 minutes.

5. Transfer chicken and squash to cutting board. Cut chicken into 1-inch-wide strips; cut each squash wedge crosswise in half.

6. To serve, on large platter, toss squash with reserved 2 tablespoons lemon marinade, then toss with chicken strips and sprinkle with chives.

Each serving: About 255 calories, 29g protein, 8g carbohydrate, 8g total fat (3g saturated), 101mg cholesterol, 240mg sodium.

Fresh chives are used to give this dish a flavor boost. The thin grasslike leaves have a mild onion flavor minus the bite. They are available year-round. For this recipe, use kitchen scissors to snip them into $1/2$-inch lengths. Store the remainder in a zip-tight plastic bag in the refrigerator for up to one week.

Five Glazes for Rotisserie Chicken

If you are the head cook in your household, you are likely to have already discovered the convenience of rotisserie chicken. And you've probably come up with at least a few ideas of your own on how to vary its presentation. Here we offer you five different glazes that can all be prepared in just a few minutes. There is something here for just about every palate. And these versatile glazes can be used for meats other than chicken. You might want to make extra Apricot-Ginger Glaze for roast ham or Honey-Mustard Glaze for pork roast.

MAKES 4 servings

Choice of glaze
1 warm rotisserie chicken (2 to 2¹/2 pounds)

Prepare choice of glaze as recipe directs. Place whole chicken on platter; using pastry brush, coat chicken all over with hot glaze. To serve, cut chicken into pieces or slices.

Apricot-Ginger Glaze

In microwave-safe small bowl, stir **2 tablespoons apricot jam, 2 tablespoons bottled horseradish,** and **¹/2 teaspoon ground ginger** until blended. Cook, uncovered, in microwave oven on High 30 seconds, stirring once.
Each serving chicken with glaze: About 365 calories, 38g protein, 8g carbohydrate, 19g total fat (5g saturated), 152mg cholesterol, 125mg sodium.

Hoisin and Five-Spice Glaze

In microwave-safe small bowl, stir **¹/4 cup hoisin sauce, 2 tablespoons soy sauce,** and **1 teaspoon Chinese five-spice powder** until blended. Cook, uncovered, in microwave oven on High 30 seconds, stirring once.
Each serving chicken with glaze: About 375 calories, 39g protein, 8g carbohydrate, 19g total fat (5g saturated), 152mg cholesterol, 860mg sodium.

Moroccan-Spiced Glaze

In microwave-safe small bowl, stir **3 tablespoons honey, 1 tablespoon fresh lemon juice, ¹/2 teaspoon ground cinnamon,** and **¹/2 teaspoon ground cumin** until blended. Cook,

uncovered, in microwave oven on High 1 minute, stirring once.
Each serving chicken with glaze: About 380 calories, 38g protein, 14g carbohydrate, 19g total fat (5g saturated), 152mg cholesterol, 115mg sodium.

Honey-Mustard Glaze

In microwave-safe small bowl, stir **2 tablespoons Dijon mustard with seeds, 2 tablespoons honey,** and **$\frac{1}{2}$ teaspoon dried thyme** (or 2 teaspoons minced fresh thyme leaves) until blended. Cook, uncovered, in microwave oven on High 30 seconds, stirring once.
Each serving chicken with glaze: About 375 calories, 39g protein, 10g carbohydrate, 19g total fat (5g saturated), 152mg cholesterol, 155mg sodium.

Balsamic-Soy Glaze

In microwave-safe bowl, stir **2 tablespoons balsamic vinegar, 2 tablespoons dark brown sugar,** and **2 tablespoons soy sauce** until blended. Cook, uncovered, in microwave oven on High 2 minutes, stirring once.
Each serving chicken with glaze: About 370 calories, 39g protein, 9g carbohydrate, 19g total fat (5g saturated), 152mg cholesterol, 605mg sodium.

Chicken Scarpariello

TOTAL TIME 20 minutes
MAKES 4 servings

A rotisserie-chicken gem, this is a perfect one-dish family supper. It has everything: color, flavor, texture, and, best of all, convenience. Sturdy poultry shears—a piece of kitchen equipment that no cook should be without—make preparation a breeze. Look for a pair with slip-proof handles. They're also good for trimming artichokes and other vegetables. After disjointing the bird, place the backbone and any other trimmings in a zip-tight bag and freeze for the stockpot.

8	ounces hot and/or sweet Italian-sausage links, cut crosswise into 1-inch pieces
3	medium garlic cloves, crushed with side of chef's knife
1	large green or red pepper, cut into 1-inch pieces
1	large onion, cut into 1-inch pieces
1	medium sprig fresh rosemary
1	tablespoon olive or vegetable oil
$1/2$	teaspoon salt
2	cups cherry or grape tomatoes
1	rotisserie chicken (2 to $2^1/2$ pounds), cut into 8 pieces, skin removed, if you like

1. Heat nonstick 12-inch skillet or 5- to 6-quart Dutch oven over medium heat 1 minute. Add sausage pieces, garlic, green pepper, onion, rosemary, oil, and salt; cover and cook, stirring occasionally, until slightly browned, about 5 minutes.

2. Stir whole cherry tomatoes into sausage mixture; arrange chicken pieces on top. Reduce heat to medium-low; cover and simmer, turning chicken pieces over halfway through cooking, until sausage is cooked through, tomato skins begin to burst, and chicken is hot, about 5 minutes longer (10 minutes if chicken has been refrigerated). Remove and discard rosemary sprig before serving.

Each serving without skin: About 495 calories, 43g protein, 12g carbohydrate, 30g total fat (9g saturated), 144mg cholesterol, 8mg sodium.

Thai Chicken with Basil

TOTAL TIME 25 minutes
MAKES 4 servings

- 1 package (10 to 12 ounces) plain couscous
- 2 teaspoons vegetable oil
- 3 garlic cloves, cut into slivers
- 2 tablespoons slivered, peeled fresh ginger
- 2 medium zucchini and/or yellow summer squashes (6 ounces each), each cut lengthwise in half, then sliced crosswise
- 1 bunch green onions, cut into 2-inch pieces
- 2 cups shredded skinless rotisserie chicken meat (10 ounces)
- 1 cup well-stirred light coconut milk (not cream of coconut)
- 2 plum tomatoes, chopped
- 1/2 teaspoon salt
- 1/2 cup loosely packed fresh basil leaves, sliced

1. Prepare couscous as label directs; set aside.

2. Meanwhile, in nonstick 12-inch skillet, heat oil over medium heat until hot. Add garlic, ginger, zucchini, and green onions; cook, stirring frequently, until vegetables are tender-crisp, 4 minutes. Transfer vegetable mixture to plate.

3. To same skillet, add chicken, coconut milk, tomatoes, and salt; heat to boiling. Return vegetable mixture to skillet; stir in basil and heat through. Serve chicken with couscous.

Each serving: About 565 calories, 34g protein, 75g carbohydrate, 14g total fat (5g saturated), 63mg cholesterol, 380mg sodium.

Coconut milk, an essential ingredient of many tropical dishes, is made by soaking grated coconut in water. Do not confuse coconut milk with canned sweetened coconut cream, or "cream of coconut," which is used for desserts and tropical drinks. Store leftover coconut milk in a jar with an airtight lid in the fridge for up to three days. Be sure to stir well before using.

Quick Chicken Mole

TOTAL TIME 25 minutes
MAKES 4 servings

2 teaspoons olive oil
1 medium onion, chopped
2 garlic cloves, crushed with garlic press
2 teaspoons chili powder
2 teaspoons unsweetened cocoa
1/4 teaspoon ground cinnamon
1 1/4 cups chicken broth
1 tablespoon creamy peanut butter
1 tablespoon tomato paste
1/4 cup golden or dark raisins
1 rotisserie chicken (2 to 2 1/2 pounds), cut into 8 pieces, skin removed, if you like
1/4 cup loosely packed fresh cilantro leaves, chopped
  cooked rice (optional)
  romaine and avocado salad (optional)
  lime wedges

Our speedy version of mole, a richly-flavored sauce with spices, nuts, and raisins, is authentic enough to satisfy any Mexican-food aficionado. If you want to serve the salad, use packaged washed and torn romaine leaves and top with thin slices of a peeled ripe avocado.

1. In nonstick 12-inch skillet, heat oil over medium heat until hot. Add onion and cook, stirring occasionally, 5 minutes. Add garlic, chili powder, cocoa, and cinnamon to skillet; cook, stirring constantly, 1 minute.

2. Stir in broth, peanut butter, and tomato paste. Add raisins; heat to boiling. Add chicken pieces to skillet. Reduce heat to medium-low; cover and simmer, turning chicken pieces halfway through cooking to coat all sides with sauce, about 5 minutes (10 minutes if chicken has been refrigerated).

3. Sprinkle chicken with cilantro. Serve chicken and sauce over rice with salad if you like. Garnish with lime wedges.

Each serving without skin: About 400 calories, 44g protein, 15g carbohydrate, 18g total fat (4g saturated), 126mg cholesterol, 475mg sodium.

Spinach and Chicken Lasagna Stacks

TOTAL TIME 30 minutes

MAKES 4 servings

This quick-fix lasagna is equally delicious with another sharp cheese, such as Cheddar or Fontina, instead of the Gruyère called for in this recipe.

7	lasagna noodles (not no-boil)
3	tablespoons butter or margarine
$1/3$	cup all-purpose flour
1	can (14 to $14^1/2$ ounces) chicken broth ($1^3/4$ cups)
$1^1/4$	cups whole milk
$1/4$	teaspoon freshly ground black pepper
$1/2$	small red pepper, cut into $1/4$-inch pieces
4	ounces Gruyère cheese, shredded (1 cup)
4	ounces fresh baby spinach leaves (4 cups)
2	cups shredded skinless rotisserie chicken meat (10 ounces)

1. In 4-quart saucepan, cook lasagna noodles as label directs. Drain.

2. Meanwhile, in 3-quart saucepan, melt butter over medium heat. With wire whisk, stir in flour until blended and smooth; cook, stirring frequently, 1 minute. Whisk in broth, milk, and black pepper; heat to boiling over high heat, stirring occasionally. Add red pepper and boil 2 minutes. Reduce heat to low. Stir in Gruyère, spinach, and chicken; heat through. Remove saucepan from heat.

3. When noodles are cool enough to handle, separate them. Cut each noodle crosswise into three equal pieces.

4. Assemble lasagna stacks: Place 1 lasagna noodle on each of 4 dinner plates. Top each with scant $1/4$ cup chicken mixture, then another noodle. Repeat with remaining chicken mixture and noodles to make 4 equal stacks, ending with chicken mixture. (You will have 1 noodle left over.)

Each serving: About 553 calories, 36g protein, 44g carbohydrate, 26g total fat (14g saturated), 114mg cholesterol, 693mg sodium.

Curried Chicken and Fruit Salad

TOTAL TIME 15 minutes

MAKES 4 servings

1/4	cup mango chutney
1/4	cup light mayonnaise
2	tablespoons fresh lime juice
2	teaspoons curry powder
2	cups (1/2-inch pieces) skinless rotisserie chicken meat (10 ounces)
2	medium stalks celery, chopped
1 1/2	cups (3/4-inch pieces) ripe cantaloupe (1/4 medium melon)
1	cup seedless red grapes, each cut in half
8	Boston lettuce leaves

A perfect main course for a sultry summer evening, this tasty salad is as easy on the cook as it is on the waistline. It's simpler to remove the skin and chop the meat while the bird is still warm, so prep it as soon as you get home. Then cover and refrigerate until you're ready to start dinner.

1. Coarsely chop any large pieces of fruit in chutney. In large bowl, combine chutney, mayonnaise, lime juice, and curry powder; stir until blended. Stir in chicken, celery, cantaloupe, and grapes.

2. To serve, divide lettuce among 4 dinner plates; top each with chicken salad.

Each serving: About 270 calories, 22g protein, 23g carbohydrate, 11g total fat (3g saturated), 68mg cholesterol, 220mg sodium.

Chicken with Lemony Egg Noodles and Peas

TOTAL TIME 30 minutes

MAKES 4 servings

This hearty one-dish meal is the perfect antidote to cold, blustery weather. Creamy and comforting, it gets a flavor boost from freshly grated lemon peel. You can use the smallest holes on a traditional box grater, or use one of the "rasp" graters that are now widely available and much more efficient. A "bald" lemon won't last long in the fridge, so squeeze the juice and store it in a tightly covered jar for another use.

8	ounces extra-wide egg noodles
4	ounces stringless sugar snap peas from 8-ounce bag
1	cup packaged shredded carrots
1	cup frozen peas
1	cup chicken broth
$1/2$	cup heavy or whipping cream
1	teaspoon freshly grated lemon peel
$1/2$	teaspoon coarsely ground black pepper
$1/2$	teaspoon salt
2	cups ($1/2$-inch pieces) skinless rotisserie chicken meat (10 ounces)

1. In large nonreactive saucepot, cook noodles as label directs. Add snap peas to pot 1 minute before noodles are done.

2. Place carrots and frozen peas in colander. Drain noodles and snap peas over carrots and peas.

3. While noodle mixture drains, in same saucepot, heat broth, cream, lemon peel, pepper, and salt to boiling over high heat. Add chicken and noodle mixture to sauce; heat through, stirring constantly.

Each serving: About 510 calories, 33g protein, 52g carbohydrate, 20g total fat (9g saturated), 158mg cholesterol, 750mg sodium.

No-Cook Barbecue Chicken Salad

TOTAL TIME 15 minutes
MAKES 4 servings

Removing kernels from the corncob may seem a daunting task, but, like many other things, it's very easy once you know how. Hold the cob upright in a shallow baking sheet, with its flat end down. With a sharp knife, slice straight down between the kernels and the cob, cutting just deep enough to release the kernels. Rotate the cob and repeat until all kernels are removed.

$^1/_4$ cup barbecue sauce
2 tablespoons cider vinegar
1 tablespoon water
2 tablespoons olive oil
1 small head romaine lettuce (about 8 ounces), cut crosswise into 1-inch slices
2 cups ($^1/_2$-inch pieces) skinless rotisserie chicken meat (10 ounces)
1 cup corn kernels cut from cobs (2 ears)
2 medium tomatoes, cut into $^1/_2$-inch pieces
1 can (15 to 19 ounces) black beans, rinsed and drained
1 can (4 to $4^1/_2$ ounces) chopped mild green chiles, drained

1. In small bowl, with wire whisk, mix barbecue sauce, vinegar, and water until blended. Whisking continuously, add oil in thin, steady stream until well blended.
2. On large deep platter, toss lettuce with $^1/_4$ cup dressing. Arrange chicken, corn, tomatoes, and beans in strips on top of lettuce. Sprinkle with chiles and drizzle with remaining dressing. Toss just before serving.

Each serving: About 350 calories, 29g protein, 36g carbohydrate, 13g total fat (3g saturated), 63mg cholesterol, 680mg sodium.

Easy Cobb Salad

TOTAL TIME 25 minutes

MAKES 6 servings

6	slices fully cooked, ready-to-serve bacon
2	bags (5 ounces each) mixed baby greens
1	pint red or yellow cherry or grape tomatoes, each cut in half
2	cups corn kernels cut from cobs (4 ears)
2	cups ($1/2$-inch cubes) skinless rotisserie chicken meat (10 ounces)
$1/2$	seedless cucumber, not peeled, finely chopped
3	ounces blue cheese, crumbled ($3/4$ cup)
$1/3$	cup bottled vinaigrette salad dressing

1. Heat bacon in microwave oven as label directs; cool slightly, then coarsely chop.

2. Line deep large platter with baby greens. Arrange cherry tomatoes, corn, chicken, cucumber, blue cheese, and bacon in striped pattern over greens. Serve with dressing.

Each serving without dressing: About 215 calories, 21g protein, 16g carbohydrate, 10g total fat (4g saturated), 49mg cholesterol, 655mg sodium.

If you're a traditionalist and have the time, you might want to add a stripe of chopped ripe avocado to this popular salad. Since avocado discolors quickly, cut and chop it just before serving or sprinkle the exposed flesh with some lemon or lime juice.

Warm Chicken Salad with Mustard-Thyme Vinaigrette

TOTAL TIME 20 minutes

MAKES 4 servings

- 3   slices bacon, each cut into $1/2$-inch pieces
- 3   green onions, thinly sliced
- $1/3$ cup cider vinegar or red wine vinegar
- 1   tablespoon olive oil
- 1   tablespoon Dijon mustard with seeds
- 2   teaspoons fresh thyme leaves
- $1/2$ teaspoon salt
- 3   cups coarsely shredded skinless rotisserie chicken meat (15 ounces)
- 1   Red Delicious, Gala, or Fuji apple, not peeled, cored and thinly sliced
- 1   bag (5 to 6 ounces) prewashed baby spinach

1. In nonstick 10-inch skillet, cook bacon over medium heat, stirring occasionally, until browned, 5 to 6 minutes. Add green onions and cook, stirring, 1 minute. Remove skillet from heat. Stir in vinegar, oil, mustard, thyme, and salt.

2. Meanwhile, in large serving bowl, toss chicken with apple and spinach until combined.

3. Pour hot dressing over chicken mixture; toss until salad is evenly coated. Serve immediately.

Each serving: About 385 calories, 29g protein, 8g carbohydrate, 27g total fat (8g saturated), 95mg cholesterol, 675mg sodium.

This hearty salad is dressed with a tangy vinaigrette that contains Dijon mustard with seeds. Unlike American-style prepared mustard, Dijon, like most European mustards, is made from brown seeds and is much zestier and more flavorful. You can substitute a good-quality American mustard, but you won't get the same bold flavor.

Texas Chicken Burgers

TOTAL TIME 30 minutes
MAKES 4 servings

Our mix of ground chicken, chopped green onions, shredded zucchini and carrot, and a hefty dose of south-western seasonings provides enough flavor to satisfy even a diehard Texan. This tasty combo is also terrific with ground turkey.

1	pound ground chicken
2	green onions, chopped
1	small zucchini (5 ounces), shredded
1	medium carrot, peeled and shredded
1	tablespoon chili powder
1/4	teaspoon ground cumin
1/8	teaspoon ground red pepper (cayenne)
3/4	teaspoon salt
1	can (16 ounces) vegetarian baked beans
1	tablespoon prepared mustard
1	tablespoon light molasses
4	whole-grain sandwich rolls, cut horizontally in half
	lettuce leaves, sliced tomato, and mustard (optional)

1. In medium bowl, with hands, combine ground chicken, green onions, zucchini, carrot, chili powder, cumin, ground red pepper, and salt just until well blended but not overmixed. On waxed paper, shape chicken mixture into four 3 1/2-inch burgers, pressing firmly; set aside.

2. In 1-quart saucepan, heat beans, mustard, and molasses to boiling over medium heat.

3. Meanwhile, spray heavy 12-inch skillet with cooking spray. Heat over medium heat until very hot but not smoking. Add burgers to skillet and cook 5 minutes. Turn burgers and cook until chicken loses its pink color throughout (internal temperature should reach 165°F), about 5 minutes longer.

4. If desired, spread bottom half of each roll with mustard. Top with lettuce and tomato slices, if using, then top with burger and top half of roll. Serve with baked beans.

Each burger with 4 ounces beans: About 429 calories, 34g protein, 51g carbohydrate, 10g total fat (3g saturated), 92mg cholesterol, 1,037mg sodium.

Buffalo Chicken Burgers

TOTAL TIME 30 minutes
MAKES 4 servings

1/4   cup light mayonnaise
1/4   cup reduced-fat sour cream
2   ounces blue cheese, crumbled (1/2 cup)
2   teaspoons cider vinegar
1/2   teaspoon Worcestershire sauce
1 1/4   pounds ground chicken or turkey
1   large stalk celery, finely chopped
3   tablespoons cayenne pepper sauce,
   plus additional for serving
   nonstick cooking spray
4   hamburger buns, split and toasted
   lettuce leaves
   carrot and celery sticks

Fans of Buffalo chicken wings will love these savory burgers, which are grilled and then served with the traditional fixin's: blue-cheese sauce and carrot and celery sticks. No need to purchase expensive imported blue cheese. A domestic variety will do, but avoid the "creamy" type; it is difficult to crumble.

1. Preheat grill pan or prepare grill for direct grilling over medium heat.

2. In small bowl, stir mayonnaise, sour cream, blue cheese, vinegar, and Worcestershire until blended; set aside. Makes about 3/4 cup.

3. In medium bowl, with hands, combine chicken, celery, and cayenne pepper sauce just until blended but not overmixed. Shape mixture into four 3/4-inch-thick burgers. Spray both sides of burgers with nonstick cooking spray.

4. Place burgers on grill over medium heat; grill, turning once, until meat loses its pink color throughout, 12 to 14 minutes. Burgers should reach an internal temperature of 165°F.

5. Serve burgers on buns with lettuce and some blue cheese sauce. Serve remaining sauce with carrot and celery sticks. Pass additional cayenne pepper sauce, if you like.

Each burger with bun: About 345 calories, 27g protein, 22g carbohydrate, 16g total fat (1g saturated), 0mg cholesterol, 785mg sodium.

Each tablespoon blue cheese sauce: About 40 calories, 1g protein, 1g carbohydrate, 4g total fat (2g saturated), 7mg cholesterol, 110mg sodium.

This Asian-style chicken soup is prepared in a flash, courtesy of ramen noodle soup mix. Sesame oil, a deep amber-colored oil pressed from toasted sesame seeds adds to its authentic flavor. Sesame oil goes rancid more quickly than vegetable oils, so buy it in small quantities and keep it in the refrigerator.

Spring Ramen Chicken Soup

TOTAL TIME 25 minutes
MAKES 4 servings

5	cups water
2	packages (3 ounces each) chicken-flavor or Oriental-flavor ramen noodle soup mix
6	ounces snow peas (about 2 cups)
2	green onions
1	large carrot, peeled
1	pound skinless, boneless chicken breasts
1	teaspoon Asian sesame oil

1. In 4-quart saucepan, heat water with seasoning packets from ramen soup mix to boiling over high heat. Meanwhile, remove strings from snow peas and cut each on diagonal in half. Slice green onions and shred carrot. Cut chicken breasts into $3/4$-inch pieces. Break ramen noodle blocks into 2 layers.
2. Add snow peas, green onions, carrot, chicken, and noodles to boiling water and cook over high heat until chicken just loses its pink color throughout, 3 to 5 minutes. Remove saucepan from heat. Stir in sesame oil.

Each serving: About 355 calories, 32g protein, 32g carbohydrate, 11g fat (4g saturated), 66mg cholesterol, 920mg sodium.

Vietnamese Rice-Noodle Soup

TOTAL TIME **30 minutes**
MAKES **4 servings**

4	ounces rice stick noodles (about $1/4$ inch wide)
3	green onions
3	cans (14 to $14^{1}/2$ ounces each) chicken broth ($5^{1}/4$ cups)
1	cup water
	3-inch piece fresh ginger, peeled and thinly sliced
$1/4$	teaspoon Chinese five-spice powder
	pinch crushed red pepper
2	cups shredded skinless rotisserie chicken meat (10 ounces)
	fresh herbs such as basil, cilantro, and mint, chopped
	lime wedges

1. Soak noodles as label directs. Drain.

2. Meanwhile, thinly slice green onions on diagonal; reserve dark green tops for garnish. In 4-quart saucepan, combine light parts of green onions with broth, water, ginger, five-spice powder, and crushed red pepper and heat to boiling over high heat. Reduce heat to low; cover and simmer 10 minutes.

3. Discard ginger, if you like. Add noodles and chicken to broth mixture; heat to boiling over high heat.

4. Ladle soup into 4 bowls; serve with chopped fresh herbs, lime wedges, and green onion tops.

Each serving: About 275 calories, 24g protein, 26g carbohydrate, 8g total fat (2g saturated), 63mg cholesterol, 1,380mg sodium.

Rice noodles, made from rice flour and water, come in various sizes, from wide, flat ribbons to thin sticks. Because they are so delicate, they can be easily overcooked and turn to mush, so follow package instructions carefully. Rice noodles are available in loose skeins or in tightly packed bundles wrapped in cellophane. Store them in a cool, dark spot for up to six months. Rice noodles are available in Asian markets and in many supermarkets.

Chicken Soup with Latin Flavors

TOTAL TIME 30 minutes
MAKES 4 servings

This is a wonderful north-of-the-border version of tortilla soup. If fresh corn is unavailable, you can substitute frozen whole-kernel corn (no need to thaw), but you will sacrifice a bit of flavor.

1	tablespoon vegetable oil
2	garlic cloves, chopped
2	medium carrots, peeled and chopped
2	medium stalks celery, chopped
1	medium onion, chopped
1/2	jalapeño chile with seeds, thinly sliced
1	teaspoon ground cumin
1	carton (32 ounces) chicken broth (4 cups)
1 1/2	cups water
1	cup corn kernels cut from cobs (2 ears)
2	tablespoons fresh lime juice
2	cups (1/2-inch pieces) skinless rotisserie chicken meat (10 ounces)
1/2	cup loosely packed fresh cilantro leaves, coarsely chopped
2	plum tomatoes, cut into 1/2-inch pieces
1	ripe medium avocado, pitted, peeled, and cut into 1/2-inch pieces
	lime wedges
	tortilla chips (optional)

1. In 6-quart saucepot, heat oil over low heat until hot. Add garlic, carrots, celery, onion, and jalapeño. Cover and cook, stirring frequently, until vegetables are tender, 8 to 10 minutes. Add cumin and cook, stirring, 30 seconds. Add broth and water; cover and heat to boiling over high heat.

2. Stir corn, lime juice, chicken pieces, and cilantro into broth mixture; heat to boiling over high heat. Remove from heat; stir in chopped tomatoes.

3. Ladle soup into 4 warm large soup bowls; sprinkle with avocado pieces. Serve with lime wedges and tortilla chips, if you like.

Each serving: About 365 calories, 27g protein, 26g carbohydrate, 19g total fat (3g saturated), 63mg cholesterol, 1,205mg sodium.

Chicken Noodle Soup

TOTAL TIME 20 minutes
MAKES 5 servings

1	carton (32 ounces) chicken broth (4 cups)
4	cups water
1	tablespoon olive oil
1	small onion, chopped
2	stalks celery, thinly sliced
2	medium carrots, peeled and thinly sliced
1/8	teaspoon freshly ground black pepper
1	pound skinless, boneless chicken breasts
3	cups medium egg noodles, uncooked (6 ounces)
1	cup frozen peas, thawed

Old-fashioned flavor with a minimum of fuss, this hearty version of the comforting favorite is a great standby when you're looking for something nourishing that doesn't require a long shopping list of ingredients or hours on the stove. Although it's not traditional, a squeeze of fresh lemon will brighten the flavors.

1. In 3-quart saucepan, heat broth and water over high heat.

2. Meanwhile, in 5- to 6-quart saucepot, heat oil over medium heat. Add onion and cook, stirring occasionally, until lightly browned, about 5 minutes. Add hot broth mixture, celery, carrots, and pepper; cover and heat to boiling over high heat.

3. While vegetables are cooking, cut chicken breasts into $3/4$-inch pieces.

4. Remove cover from saucepot. Stir in noodles; cover and cook 3 minutes. Stir in peas and chicken pieces; cover and heat to boiling. Reduce heat and simmer 3 to 4 minutes.

Each serving: About 305 calories, 30g protein, 33g carbohydrate, 6g total fat (1g saturated), 85mg cholesterol, 615mg sodium.

Hot-and-Sour Soup

TOTAL TIME 30 minutes

MAKES 4 servings

This versatile Chinese soup can be served as is as a first or main course, or add thinly sliced cooked chicken or pork to turn it into a hearty cold-weather meal.

1   tablespoon vegetable oil
4   ounces shiitake mushrooms, stems removed and caps thinly sliced
3   tablespoons reduced-sodium soy sauce
1   package (15 ounces) extrafirm tofu, drained, patted dry, and cut into 1-inch cubes
2   tablespoons cornstarch
1   cup water
1   carton (32 ounces) chicken broth (4 cups)
3   tablespoons seasoned rice vinegar
2   tablespoons grated, peeled fresh ginger
1   tablespoon Worcestershire sauce
$1/2$ teaspoon Asian sesame oil
$1/4$ teaspoon ground red pepper (cayenne)
2   large eggs, beaten
2   green onions, sliced

1. In nonstick 5-quart saucepot, heat vegetable oil over medium heat until hot. Add mushrooms, soy sauce, and tofu; cook, gently stirring often, until liquid has evaporated, 5 minutes.

2. In cup, with fork, blend cornstarch with $1/4$ cup water until smooth; set aside. Add broth and remaining $3/4$ cup water to tofu mixture; heat to boiling. Stir in cornstarch mixture and boil, stirring, 30 seconds. Reduce heat to medium-low; add vinegar, ginger, Worcestershire, sesame oil, and ground red pepper; simmer 5 minutes.

3. Remove saucepot from heat. Slowly pour beaten eggs into soup in thin, steady stream around edge of saucepot. Carefully stir the soup once in circular motion so egg separates into strands. Sprinkle with green onions and serve hot.

Each serving: About 280 calories, 18g protein, 17g carbohydrate, 15g total fat (3g saturated), 106mg cholesterol, 1,790mg sodium.

Turkey-Cutlet Pockets
with Marinated Tomatoes

TOTAL TIME 30 minutes

MAKES 4 servings

3	large tomatoes, each cut into $1/2$-inch-thick slices
$1/2$	small red onion, thinly sliced
2	tablespoons balsamic vinegar
2	tablespoons extra-virgin olive oil
	pinch sugar
$1/2$	teaspoon salt
$1/2$	teaspoon freshly ground black pepper
$1/4$	cup loosely packed fresh basil leaves, thinly sliced, plus 8 large basil leaves
4	turkey breast cutlets (1 pound)
8	oil-packed dried tomato halves, thinly sliced
4	thin slices Fontina or mozzarella cheese (about 2 ounces)
	toothpicks

Convenient turkey cutlets are paired with a tangy Italian medley of dried tomatoes, Fontina cheese, and fresh basil. If you prefer, you can substitute roasted red peppers for the dried tomatoes. Just be sure to rinse them under cold water and pat them dry before slicing.

1. Prepare grill for covered direct grilling over medium heat.

2. Layer fresh tomato slices and onion in concentric circles on large platter. In cup, with fork, mix vinegar, oil, sugar, $1/4$ teaspoon salt, and $1/4$ teaspoon pepper until blended; drizzle dressing over tomatoes and onions. Sprinkle salad with sliced basil. Set aside at room temperature.

3. If turkey breast cutlets are not uniformly thin, with meat mallet, or between two sheets of plastic wrap or waxed paper with rolling pin, pound cutlets to even $1/4$-inch thickness.

4. On half of each turkey cutlet, place 2 whole basil leaves, one-fourth of dried tomatoes, and 1 slice Fontina. Fold each cutlet over to enclose filling; secure with toothpicks. Sprinkle cutlets with remaining $1/4$ teaspoon salt and $1/4$ teaspoon pepper.

5. Place cutlets on grill over medium heat; cover and cook 5 to 6 minutes. With tongs, turn and grill until juices run clear when cutlets are pierced with tip of knife, 5 to 6 minutes longer.

6. Transfer cutlets to plates; remove toothpicks. Serve with tomato salad. Drizzle any vinaigrette on platter over cutlets.

Each serving: About 300 calories, 31g protein, 10g carbohydrate, 15g total fat (5g saturated), 75mg cholesterol, 485mg sodium.

Turkey Cutlets with Pears and Tarragon

TOTAL TIME 25 minutes
MAKES 4 servings

1	tablespoon olive oil
4	turkey breast cutlets (about 1 pound)
1/4	teaspoon salt
1/8	teaspoon freshly ground black pepper
2	large firm, ripe pears, peeled, cored, and cut into 1/2-inch-thick wedges
1	cup chicken broth
1/4	cup dried tart cherries or cranberries
2	tablespoons Dijon mustard with seeds
1/2	teaspoon dried tarragon
1	bag (9 ounces) ready-to-microwave-in-bag spinach

1. In 12-inch skillet, heat oil over high heat until hot. Sprinkle turkey breast cutlets with salt and pepper. Add cutlets to skillet and cook, turning once, until golden brown on both sides and they just lose their pink color throughout, 3 to 4 minutes. Transfer cutlets to plate; keep warm.

2. To same skillet, add pears. Reduce heat to medium-high and cook pears, turning occasionally, until browned, about 3 minutes. Add broth, cherries, Dijon mustard, and tarragon to skillet. Increase heat to high and cook, stirring occasionally, until sauce thickens slightly and pears are tender, 4 to 5 minutes.

3. Meanwhile, in microwave oven, cook spinach in bag as label directs.

4. Return cutlets to skillet; heat through, spooning pear sauce over cutlets.

5. To serve, spoon spinach onto 4 dinner plates. Top with turkey, pears, and sauce.

Each serving: About 255 calories, 31g protein, 20g carbohydrate, 6g total fat (1g saturated), 71mg cholesterol, 565mg sodium.

Pears are available year-round but are at their peak in autumn. There are a number of different varieties that range in color, shape, texture, and flavor. The best pears for this recipe are Anjou and Bosc, which are juicy and keep their shape when cooked. Peel and cut the pears just before you are ready to use them; like cut apples, they discolor. If you want to prep them in advance, place them in a bowl of cold water to which you've added 1 teaspoon lemon juice. Drain and pat dry before using.

155

Turkey Cutlets with Nectarine-Arugula Salad

TOTAL TIME 25 minutes
MAKES 4 servings

Nectarines, like peaches, are members of the stone-fruit family. Although they closely resemble peaches, they are not hybrids. However, like peaches, nectarines do discolor. So prepare them while the cutlets are grilling, then add them to the dressing.

1 lemon
2 tablespoons olive oil
1 small shallot, minced (about 1 tablespoon)
1 teaspoon Dijon mustard with seeds
1 teaspoon honey
3/4 teaspoon salt
1/4 teaspoon freshly ground black pepper
4 turkey breast cutlets (1 pound)
1 pound nectarines, pitted and cut into
    1/2-inch-thick wedges
1 bag (5 ounces) baby arugula

1. Lightly grease grill rack. Prepare grill for direct grilling over medium-high heat.

2. From lemon, grate 1 teaspoon peel and squeeze 1 tablespoon juice. In large bowl, with wire whisk, mix lemon juice, oil, shallot, mustard, honey, 1/4 teaspoon salt, and 1/8 teaspoon pepper.

3. Sprinkle turkey breast cutlets with lemon peel and remaining 1/2 teaspoon salt and 1/8 teaspoon pepper. Place cutlets on grill over medium-high heat; grill, turning once, until turkey loses its pink color throughout, 4 to 5 minutes. Transfer to warm plate.

4. Add nectarines and arugula to dressing in bowl; gently toss to mix well. Pile arugula salad on large platter and top with cutlets.

Each serving: About 245 calories, 28g protein, 16g carbohydrate, 8g total fat (1g saturated), 71mg cholesterol, 500mg sodium.

Turkey Cutlets, Indian Style

TOTAL TIME 20 minutes
MAKES 6 servings

2	large limes
1/3	cup plain low-fat yogurt
1	tablespoon vegetable oil
1	tablespoon minced, peeled fresh ginger
1	teaspoon ground cumin
1	teaspoon ground coriander
1	teaspoon salt
1	garlic clove, crushed with garlic press
1 1/2	pounds turkey breast cutlets

1. Prepare grill for direct grilling over medium heat.

2. Meanwhile, from 1 lime, grate 1 teaspoon peel and squeeze 1 tablespoon juice. Cut remaining lime into wedges; set aside.

3. In large bowl, mix lime peel, lime juice, yogurt, oil, ginger, cumin, coriander, salt, and garlic until blended.

4. Just before grilling, add turkey breast cutlets to bowl with yogurt mixture; stir to coat. (Do not let cutlets marinate in yogurt mixture; their texture will become mealy.)

5. Place cutlets on grill over medium heat and grill, turning once, until they just lose their pink color throughout, 5 to 7 minutes. Serve with lime wedges.

Each serving: About 160 calories, 29g protein, 3g carbohydrate, 3g total fat (1g saturated), 71mg cholesterol, 450mg sodium.

Company coming? Turn this quick dish into an Indian feast: Set out bowls of tangy yogurt, store-bought mango chutney, basmati rice, wedges of fresh lime, and chopped fresh cilantro, and let everyone help themselves.

Spinach-Stuffed Turkey Scaloppine

TOTAL TIME 30 minutes

MAKES 4 servings

Easy, but elegant enough for company, our take on an Italian classic uses thin turkey breast slices instead of pricey veal scallopine. Add a pinch of nutmeg to the flour mixture in step one for a subtle hint of sweetness.

1 package (14 to 16 ounces) thin turkey breast slices for scaloppine
1 package (3 ounces) thinly sliced prosciutto
1 1/2 cups loosely packed prewashed spinach leaves, tough stems trimmed
toothpicks
2 teaspoons all-purpose flour
1/2 teaspoon coarsely ground black pepper
1 tablespoon olive oil
1 cup low-sodium chicken broth

1. Place turkey breast slices on waxed paper. Top each slice with prosciutto, cutting slices to fit, then top with spinach leaves. Roll turkey jelly-roll fashion to enclose filling; secure with toothpicks if necessary. Sprinkle rolls with flour and pepper. If not cooking rolls right away, transfer to plate; cover with plastic wrap and refrigerate up to 4 hours.

2. When ready to cook rolls, in nonstick 12-inch skillet, heat oil over medium heat until hot but not smoking. Add rolls and cook, turning frequently, until browned on all sides, 6 to 7 minutes. Cover and cook, turning once, until turkey just loses its pink color throughout, about 7 minutes longer. Transfer rolls to plate. Cover loosely with foil to keep warm.

3. Add chicken broth to drippings in skillet; heat to boiling over medium heat. Boil until broth thickens slightly and is reduced to about 1/3 cup, 4 to 5 minutes. Remove toothpicks from turkey rolls. Serve rolls with sauce.

Each serving: About 215 calories, 35g protein, 2g carbohydrate, 6g total fat (2g saturated), 86mg cholesterol, 680mg sodium.

Turkey Cutlets with Melon Salsa

TOTAL TIME 25 minutes
MAKES 4 servings

Our refreshing sweet-hot fruit salsa calls for a crisp, mild-flavored Kirby—a small, immature cucumber mostly used for pickling. You can substitute a firm regular cucumber. First scrub it to remove any wax from the skin, cut crosswise in half, scoop out the seeds, and shred. The well-wrapped leftover cucumber will keep in the refrigerator up to five days.

2 limes
1^1/$_2$ cups chopped cantaloupe
1^1/$_2$ cups chopped honeydew melon
1 small Kirby (pickling) cucumber, shredded (^{1}/$_2$ cup)
1 jalapeño chile, seeded and finely chopped
^{1}/$_4$ cup loosely packed fresh basil leaves, chopped
^{1}/$_4$ teaspoon salt
^{1}/$_4$ teaspoon coarsely ground black pepper
4 turkey breast cutlets (1 pound)
4 ounces thinly sliced prosciutto

1. Grease grill rack. Prepare grill for direct grilling over medium heat.

2. From 1 lime, grate 1 teaspoon peel and squeeze 2 tablespoons juice. Cut remaining lime into 4 wedges and set aside.

3. In medium bowl, toss cantaloupe, melon, cucumber, jalapeño, and basil with lime juice and salt. Set aside. Makes about 3 cups salsa.

4. Sprinkle turkey breast cutlets with lime peel and pepper. Wrap each cutlet with 1 slice prosciutto, pressing firmly to adhere. Place cutlets on grill over medium heat; grill, turning once, until turkey loses its pink color throughout, 5 to 7 minutes. Transfer turkey to plate; serve with melon salsa and lime wedges.

Each serving turkey only: About 185 calories, 35g protein, 0g carbohydrate, 4g total fat (1g saturated), 86mg cholesterol, 815mg sodium.

Each ^{1}/$_4$ cup salsa: About 10 calories, 0g protein, 3g carbohydrate, 0g total fat, 0mg cholesterol, 50mg sodium.

Turkey Cakes
with Chipotle Mayonnaise

TOTAL TIME 30 minutes
MAKES 4 servings

1	green onion, cut into 1-inch pieces
3/4	cup loosely packed fresh cilantro leaves
1	cup leftover mashed potatoes
12	ounces leftover turkey, skin removed, cut into large pieces (about 3 cups)
1	tablespoon all-purpose flour
2	tablespoons plus 1 teaspoon vegetable oil
1	garlic clove, crushed with garlic press
1	can (15 to 19 ounces) black beans, rinsed and drained
1	cup frozen whole-kernel corn
2	tablespoons fresh lime juice
1/3	cup light mayonnaise
2	teaspoons hot pepper sauce with chipotle or adobo puree
	lime wedges (optional)

1. In food processor with knife blade attached, pulse onion and 1/2 cup cilantro six times. Add potatoes and turkey; pulse five to seven times, scraping side of processor with rubber spatula to combine (turkey should be chunky). Shape by 1/3 cupfuls into eight 3-inch patties; dust with flour.

2. In nonstick 12-inch skillet, heat 2 tablespoons oil over medium heat. Add turkey cakes; cook, turning once, until golden on both sides, 10 to 12 minutes.

3. Meanwhile, in 1-quart saucepan, heat remaining 1 teaspoon oil over medium heat. Add garlic; cook, stirring, 30 seconds. Stir in beans and corn; heat through. Stir in lime juice and remaining 1/4 cup cilantro leaves.

4. In cup, stir mayonnaise and hot pepper sauce until blended. Serve turkey cakes with chipotle mayonnaise, bean salad, and lime wedges, if you like.

Each serving turkey cakes with chipotle mayonnaise: About 330 calories, 32g protein, 13g carbohydrate, 16g total fat (2g saturated), 105mg cholesterol, 395mg sodium.

Each serving bean salad: About 120 calories, 7g protein, 26g carbohydrate, 2g total fat (0g saturated), 0mg cholesterol, 280mg sodium.

If you roasted a behemoth turkey for your family and are now up to your chin in leftovers, this recipe is one you must try! A delicious southwestern take on crab cakes, this dish gets its punch from adobo, the thick, vinegary sauce canned with chipotle chiles. It is available in Latin markets and in some supermarkets in the ethnic foods section. Use leftover adobo to flavor and thicken stews and sauces. A little bit goes a long way, so add a bit at a time, tasting as you go.

Crispy Duck Breasts with Tart Cherry Sauce

TOTAL TIME 30 minutes
MAKES 4 servings

This streamlined classic recipe is also great made with pork. You can substitute two $3/4$-inch-thick (6 ounces) boneless pork loin chops for the duck. In Step 1, season the chops and cook them in 1 teaspoon vegetable oil over medium heat, for about 8 minutes, turning them once. Then proceed as directed.

1	package (6 ounces) white-and-wild rice blend, cooked (optional)
4	small duck breast halves (6 ounces each)
$1/2$	teaspoon salt
$1/2$	teaspoon freshly ground black pepper
$2/3$	cup port wine
2	cans ($14 1/2$ ounces) tart cherries in water, well drained
$1/4$	cup sugar
	steamed green beans (optional)

1. Prepare rice as label directs. Keep warm.

2. Meanwhile, pat duck breasts dry with paper towels. Make several $1/4$-inch-deep diagonal slashes in duck skin. Place breasts, skin side down, in nonstick 10-inch skillet; sprinkle with salt and pepper. Cook over medium heat until skin is deep brown, about 12 minutes; turn breasts and cook 3 minutes longer for medium. Transfer breasts, skin side down, to cutting board; let stand 5 minutes for easier slicing. Discard fat from skillet but do not wash.

3. While duck is standing, add port to skillet; heat to boiling over medium heat. Boil until reduced by half, about 5 minutes. Add cherries and sugar and simmer, stirring occasionally, until most of liquid has evaporated, 3 to 4 minutes.

4. To serve, slice breasts crosswise. Transfer slices, skin side up, to 4 dinner plates. Spoon cherry sauce over duck. Serve with rice and green beans, if you like.

Each serving without rice or green beans: About 320 calories, 23g protein, 36g carbohydrate, 10g total fat (3g saturated), 120mg cholesterol, 380mg sodium.

CHAPTER 3

Fish & Shellfish

Cornstarch has nearly twice the thickening power of flour with a bonus—it leaves the liquid mixture clear rather than cloudy; cornstarch must be dissolved into a small amount of liquid, like wine or broth, or, as in this case, the stir-fry sauce, before it is added to a dish and then brought to a boil and cooked for a minute or two.

Shrimp and Pineapple Stir-fry

TOTAL TIME 20 minutes
MAKES 4 servings

1	cup quick-cooking brown rice
2	teaspoons vegetable oil
1	bag (16 ounces) fresh mixed cut vegetables (broccoli, carrots, sugar snap peas, and celery blend)
1/3	cup bottled stir-fry sauce
2	teaspoons cornstarch
1	pound frozen large raw shelled and deveined shrimp
1	can (8 ounces) pineapple chunks in juice

1. Prepare rice as label directs.

2. Meanwhile, in nonstick 12-inch skillet, heat oil over medium heat until hot. Add vegetables and cook, stirring frequently (stir-frying), until evenly coated with oil. Cover skillet and cook, stirring occasionally, until vegetables are tender-crisp, 3 to 4 minutes.

3. In cup, blend stir-fry sauce and cornstarch until smooth. Add shrimp, pineapple with its juice, and stir-fry sauce mixture to vegetables in skillet and cook, stirring occasionally, just until shrimp turn opaque throughout, 4 to 5 minutes. Serve over rice.

Each serving: About 310 calories, 27g protein, 41g carbohydrate, 5g total fat (1g saturated), 162mg cholesterol, 895mg sodium.

Shrimp Scampi

TOTAL TIME 15 minutes

MAKES 4 servings

2	tablespoons butter or margarine
1	pound large shrimp, shelled and deveined, leaving tail part of shell on, if you like
2	garlic cloves, crushed with garlic press
1/4	teaspoon crushed red pepper
1/4	teaspoon salt
1/4	cup loosely packed fresh parsley leaves, chopped lemon wedges

In 12-inch skillet, melt butter over medium-high heat. Add shrimp, garlic, crushed red pepper, and salt; cook, stirring frequently, just until shrimp turn opaque throughout, about 3 minutes. Sprinkle with chopped parsley; serve with lemon wedges.

Each serving: About 175 calories, 23g protein, 2g carbohydrate, 8g total fat (4g saturated), 188mg cholesterol, 373mg sodium.

Like many Italian classics, this simple dish is prepared to underscore rather than embellish the freshness of the ingredients. If you prefer, you can substitute an equal amount of sea scallops or squid for the shrimp, or stir in chopped plum tomatoes or a cup of frozen peas. Serve with crusty bread and a Romaine salad.

Citrus Shrimp

TOTAL TIME **20 minutes**
MAKES **4 servings**

Adding fruit to savory dishes creates a whole new taste dimension. In this recipe we flavor the shrimp with freshly grated orange peel and juice and extend the theme by adding orange slices to the couscous. Substitute half a coarsely chopped red or yellow pepper for the peas, if you prefer.

3	navel oranges
1 1/2	cups water
1	cup whole-wheat couscous
1/2	teaspoon salt
1/4	teaspoon freshly ground black pepper
1	tablespoon olive oil
1	pound large shrimp, shelled and deveined, with tail part of shell left on, if you like
1	cup frozen peas, thawed
2	tablespoons finely chopped red onion

1. From 1 orange, grate 1 teaspoon peel and squeeze 1/2 cup juice. Peel remaining 2 oranges; cut each orange horizontally into thin slices, then cut each slice in half. Set aside.

2. In 1-quart saucepan, heat water to boiling over high heat. Stir in couscous, salt, and 1/8 teaspoon pepper. Cover saucepan and remove from heat; let stand 5 minutes.

3. Meanwhile, in nonstick 12-inch skillet, heat oil over medium heat until very hot but not smoking. Stir in shrimp, orange peel and juice, and remaining 1/8 teaspoon pepper. Cook shrimp, stirring occasionally, until opaque throughout, 3 to 4 minutes.

4. With fork, fluff couscous; transfer to large bowl. Stir in peas, onion, and reserved orange slices. Serve couscous with shrimp.

Each serving: About 405 calories, 30g protein, 61g carbohydrate, 6g total fat (1g saturated), 140mg cholesterol, 470mg sodium.

Sesame Shrimp and Asparagus

TOTAL TIME 25 minutes
MAKES 4 servings

1	cup jasmine rice
1/8	teaspoon salt
4	teaspoons olive oil
1 1/2	teaspoons Asian sesame oil
2	pounds asparagus, trimmed
1/4	cup reduced-sodium soy sauce
2	teaspoons seasoned rice vinegar
1	large green onion, chopped
1	pound large shrimp, shelled and deveined
1/8	teaspoon crushed red pepper

1. Preheat oven to 450°F. Prepare rice as label directs.

2. Meanwhile, in cup, with fork, stir salt, 2 teaspoons olive oil, and 1 teaspoon sesame oil until blended. In jelly-roll pan, toss asparagus with oil mixture; roast until tender, 10 to 12 minutes.

3. In small bowl, with wire whisk, mix soy sauce, vinegar, green onion, and remaining 1/2 teaspoon sesame oil; set aside.

4. In nonstick 12-inch skillet, heat remaining 2 teaspoons olive oil over medium heat until very hot. Add shrimp and sprinkle with crushed red pepper; cook, stirring frequently, until opaque throughout, about 3 minutes.

5. Transfer shrimp, asparagus, and rice to dinner plates; drizzle with dressing.

Each serving: About 370 calories, 27g protein, 44g carbohydrate, 9g total fat (1g saturated), 140mg cholesterol, 850mg sodium.

These days most supermarkets stock a good selection of commercially cultivated rice. This recipe calls for jasmine rice, a popular long-grain variety that yields fluffy grains that remain separate. If you like, you can substitute basmati rice, a highly aromatic long-grain variety with a sweet, nutty flavor. If neither is available, plain long-grain white rice is also a good option.

Shrimp and Tomato Summer Salad

TOTAL TIME 25 minutes
MAKES 6 servings

Want to enjoy this light but satisfying dinner salad year-round? Just use 2^1/$_2$ pounds plum tomatoes or 1^1/$_2$ pints cherry tomatoes, halved.

2	tablespoons olive oil
2	tablespoons red wine vinegar
^{3}/$_4$	teaspoon salt
^{1}/$_4$	teaspoon coarsely ground black pepper
^{1}/$_2$	cup loosely packed fresh parsley leaves, chopped
^{1}/$_4$	cup loosely packed fresh mint leaves, thinly sliced
1	pound cooked shelled and deveined large shrimp
2^1/$_2$	pounds ripe tomatoes (4 large), cut into 1-inch pieces
1	English (seedless) cucumber or 4 Kirby cucumbers, cut lengthwise into quarters, then cut crosswise into 1-inch pieces
1	small red onion, chopped
2	ounces feta cheese, crumbled (about ^{1}/$_2$ cup)

In serving bowl, with wire whisk, mix oil, vinegar, salt, and pepper until blended; stir in parsley and mint. Add shrimp, tomatoes, cucumber, and onion to dressing in bowl; stir to combine. Sprinkle salad with feta and serve at room temperature or cover and refrigerate to serve later.

Each serving: About 200 calories, 20g protein, 13g carbohydrate, 8g total fat (2g saturated), 156mg cholesterol, 585mg sodium.

Cajun Shrimp with Remoulade Sauce

TOTAL TIME 30 minutes

MAKES 4 servings

Remoulade Sauce

1/2	cup light mayonnaise
2	tablespoons ketchup
2	tablespoons finely chopped celery
1	green onion, finely chopped
1	tablespoon Dijon mustard with seeds
1	tablespoon finely chopped fresh parsley
2	teaspoons fresh lemon juice
1/2	teaspoon Cajun seasoning

Cajun Shrimp

1	tablespoon Cajun seasoning
1	tablespoon olive oil
2	teaspoons freshly grated lemon peel
1 1/4	pounds large shrimp, shelled and deveined, leaving tail part of shell on, if you like
	lemon wedges (optional)

Cajun seasoning is a heady blend of garlic, onion, chiles, peppers, and herbs. Here it is used to season the shrimp and kick up the remoulade, the traditional French mayonnaise-based sauce used to accompany meat, fish, and shellfish.

1. Prepare sauce: In small bowl, mix mayonnaise, ketchup, celery, green onion, Dijon mustard, parsley, lemon juice, and Cajun seasoning. Cover and refrigerate up to 3 days if not serving right away. Makes about 1 cup.

2. Prepare grill for direct grilling over medium-high heat.

3. Prepare shrimp: In medium bowl, mix Cajun seasoning, oil, and lemon peel. Add shrimp to spice mixture and toss until evenly coated. Place shrimp on grill over medium-high heat and grill, turning once, until shrimp are just opaque throughout, 3 to 4 minutes.

4. Transfer shrimp to platter. Serve with lemon wedges, if you like, and remoulade sauce.

Each serving shrimp: About 155 calories, 24g protein, 2g carbohydrate, 5g total fat (1g saturated), 175mg cholesterol, 575mg sodium.

Each 1 tablespoon sauce: About 30 calories, 0g protein, 2g carbohydrate, 3g total fat (1g saturated), 3mg cholesterol, 95mg sodium.

Shrimp with Asian Barbecue Sauce

TOTAL TIME 20 minutes
MAKES 4 servings

This delicious barbecue sauce is also great on pork ribs. So save yourself some time and energy and double the sauce ingredients. Store the extra sauce in an airtight jar in the refrigerator for up to one week. When you're ready to prepare those ribs, just substitute your premade sauce for the one called for in your recipe.

	romaine lettuce leaves
$1^1/4$	pounds large shrimp, shelled and deveined, leaving tail part of shell on, if you like
4	(10- to 12-inch) skewers
$1/3$	cup hoisin sauce
3	tablespoons ketchup
$1^1/2$	teaspoons grated, peeled fresh ginger
$1/4$	teaspoon Chinese five-spice powder
2	tablespoons rice vinegar
2	tablespoons water

1. Lightly grease grill rack. Prepare grill for direct grilling over medium heat.

2. Arrange lettuce on platter and set aside. Thread shrimp onto skewers.

3. In small bowl, stir hoisin sauce, ketchup, ginger, five-spice powder, and 1 tablespoon vinegar until blended. Transfer $1/4$ cup barbecue sauce to another small bowl. Stir in water and remaining 1 tablespoon vinegar; set aside to serve as dipping sauce.

4. Brush shrimp with some barbecue sauce. Place shrimp on grill over medium heat and cook 2 minutes. Brush shrimp with sauce. Turn and brush with remaining sauce; grill until opaque throughout, 1 to 2 minutes longer. Transfer skewers to lettuce-lined platter and serve with dipping sauce.

Each serving: About 185 calories, 25g protein, 13g carbohydrate, 3g total fat (1g saturated), 175mg cholesterol, 540mg sodium.

Shrimp and Scallop Kabobs

TOTAL TIME 25 minutes
MAKES 6 servings

1   pound large shrimp, shelled and deveined, leaving tail
      part of shell on, if you like
1   pound large sea scallops
3   tablespoons soy sauce
3   tablespoons seasoned rice vinegar
2   tablespoons grated, peeled fresh ginger
1   tablespoon brown sugar
1   tablespoon Asian sesame oil
2   garlic cloves, crushed with garlic press
1   bunch green onions, cut on diagonal into
      3-inch-long pieces
12 cherry tomatoes
6   (12-inch) metal skewers

Get a jumpstart on dinner by making the soy-sauce mixture a day ahead and refrigerate it in an airtight container overnight. When ready to use, whisk the mixture to recombine ingredients before adding the shrimp and scallops.

1. Prepare grill for direct grilling over medium heat.

2. Rinse shrimp with cold running water. Pat shrimp and scallops dry with paper towels.

3. In large bowl, mix soy sauce, vinegar, ginger, brown sugar, sesame oil, and garlic. Add shrimp and scallops; toss until evenly coated.

4. Alternately thread shrimp, scallops, green onions, and cherry tomatoes onto metal skewers. Place skewers on grill over medium heat; grill shrimp and scallops, turning skewers occasionally and basting with any remaining soy-sauce mixture halfway through cooking, until just opaque throughout, 6 to 8 minutes.

Each serving: About 185 calories, 26g protein, 10g carbohydrate, 4g total fat (1g saturated), 118mg cholesterol, 880mg sodium.

Grilled Shrimp with Black Beans

TOTAL TIME 20 minutes
MAKES 4 servings

Whenever you use canned beans, always give them a quick rinse under cold water and drain them. This will refresh their flavor and removes some of the sodium added during the canning process.

3 limes
2 cans (15 to 19 ounces each) black beans, rinsed and drained
2 ripe plum tomatoes (8 ounces), chopped
2 green onions, thinly sliced
1 small yellow pepper, seeded and chopped
1 jalapeño chile, seeded and finely chopped
1/2 cup loosely packed fresh cilantro leaves, chopped
1 tablespoon olive oil
3/4 teaspoon salt
1 pound large shrimp, shelled and deveined, leaving tail part of shell on, if you like

1. Prepare grill for direct grilling over medium-high heat.

2. Meanwhile, from 1 lime, grate 1/2 teaspoon peel and squeeze 2 tablespoons juice. Cut remaining limes into wedges and set aside. In large bowl, stir lime juice and 1/4 teaspoon lime peel with beans, tomatoes, green onions, yellow pepper, jalapeño, cilantro, oil, and 1/2 teaspoon salt. Set aside at room temperature. Makes about 5 cups.

3. In medium bowl, toss shrimp with remaining 1/4 teaspoon lime peel and 1/4 teaspoon salt. Place shrimp on grill over medium-high heat and grill, turning once, until opaque throughout, 3 to 4 minutes.

4. Stir about one-half of shrimp into bean salad; top with remaining shrimp. Serve with lime wedges.

Each serving: About 290 calories, 31g protein, 41g carbohydrate, 5g total fat (1g saturated), 180mg cholesterol, 890mg sodium.

Seared Scallop Salad with Basil Vinaigrette

TOTAL TIME 15 minutes
MAKES 4 servings

1 can (15 to 19 ounces) white kidney beans (cannellini), rinsed and drained
2 tablespoons fresh lemon juice
1/2 cup loosely packed fresh basil leaves, chopped
3 tablespoons olive oil
3/4 teaspoon salt
1 pound sea scallops
1/4 teaspoon coarsely ground black pepper
1 bag (4 to 5 ounces) mesclun or baby salad greens (3 to 4 cups)

1. In large bowl, toss beans with lemon juice, basil, 2 tablespoons oil, and 1/4 teaspoon salt; set aside.

2. In 12-inch skillet, heat remaining 1 tablespoon oil over medium-high heat until very hot but not smoking. Meanwhile, pull tough crescent-shaped muscle, if any, from side of each scallop.

3. Add scallops to skillet; sprinkle with pepper and remaining 1/2 teaspoon salt. Cook scallops, turning once, just until opaque throughout, 4 to 5 minutes.

4. To serve, toss mesclun with bean mixture and arrange on dinner plates; top with scallops.

Each serving: About 300 calories, 25g protein, 23g carbohydrate, 12g total fat (2g saturated), 37mg cholesterol, 795mg sodium.

If you've never shopped for scallops before, look for those that are creamy pink. Avoid any that are very white and plump; they may have been soaked in a preservative solution. Soaked scallops also tend to expel a lot of liquid while cooking and won't brown nicely.

Seared Scallops with Saffron Couscous

TOTAL TIME 30 minutes

MAKES 4 servings

Saffron, which is used to flavor a variety of Mediterranean dishes, has a fabulous earthy flavor with a subtle bite. It's available as threads or as powder. Thread saffron, while pricey, is best; you won't need to use much. Powdered saffron on the other hand, is often mixed with other ingredients to extend it, so it lacks the same flavorful punch.

1	large lemon
1	bottle (8 ounces) clam juice
$1/4$	cup water
$1/2$	cup grape tomatoes, each cut in half
1	ounce fully cooked chorizo, cut lengthwise in half, then crosswise into $1/4$-inch-thick pieces (about $1/4$ cup)
$1/4$	teaspoon saffron threads, crumbled
1	package (10 ounces) frozen peas
1	cup couscous
$1/2$	teaspoon salt
1	pound sea scallops
$1/4$	teaspoon coarsely ground black pepper
1	tablespoon olive oil

1. From lemon, grate 2 teaspoons peel and squeeze 2 tablespoons juice.

2. In 3-quart saucepan, heat clam juice, water, tomatoes, chorizo, and saffron to boiling over high heat. Stir in peas; heat to boiling. Remove saucepan from heat; stir in couscous, 1 teaspoon lemon peel, and $1/4$ teaspoon salt. Cover and let stand 5 minutes.

3. Meanwhile, pull tough crescent-shaped muscle, if any, from side of each scallop. Pat scallops dry with paper towels. In medium bowl, toss scallops with $1/4$ teaspoon pepper and remaining $1/4$ teaspoon salt and 1 teaspoon lemon peel.

4. In 12-inch skillet, heat oil over medium-high heat until very hot. Add scallops; cook, turning once, until browned and opaque throughout, 5 to 6 minutes.

5. Remove skillet from heat; stir in lemon juice. Fluff couscous mixture with fork and serve with scallops.

Each serving: About 400 calories, 31g protein, 50g carbohydrate, 8g total fat (2g saturated), 44mg cholesterol, 790mg sodium.

Orzo and Scallops with Tomato Cream Sauce

TOTAL TIME **30 minutes**
MAKES **6 servings**

While not as tender as their smaller bay scallop cousins, sea scallops are still sweet and moist, and because they are more widely available, they are also less expensive.

1	package (16 ounces) orzo pasta
4	slices bacon, cut into $1/2$-inch pieces
1	medium onion, chopped
1	pound sea scallops
1	can ($14^1/2$ ounces) diced tomatoes
1	cup frozen peas
$1/4$	cup heavy or whipping cream
$1/4$	teaspoon coarsely ground black pepper

1. In large saucepot, cook pasta as label directs. Drain.

2. Meanwhile, in 12-inch skillet, cook bacon over medium heat until almost browned. Add onion; cook until softened, about 5 minutes. With slotted spoon, transfer bacon and onion to medium bowl.

3. While bacon is cooking, pull off tough crescent-shaped muscle, if any, from side of each scallop. Pat scallops dry with paper towels.

4. Discard all but 1 tablespoon bacon drippings from skillet. Increase heat to high; add scallops and cook, turning once, just until they turn opaque throughout and are lightly browned on both sides, 3 to 4 minutes. Transfer scallops with any liquid to bowl with bacon mixture.

5. To same skillet, add tomatoes with their juice, frozen peas, cream, and pepper; heat to boiling over medium-high heat, stirring frequently. Return scallop mixture to skillet; heat through.

6. To serve, spoon scallop mixture over pasta.

Each serving: About 470 calories, 25g protein, 65g carbohydrate, 12g total fat (4g saturated), 42mg cholesterol, 730mg sodium.

Garlicky Grilled Clams and Mussels

TOTAL TIME 30 minutes
MAKES 4 servings

4	tablespoons butter or margarine, cut into pieces
2	tablespoons olive oil
3	garlic cloves, finely chopped
1	large shallot, finely chopped ($1/4$ cup)
$1/2$	cup dry white wine
$1/4$	teaspoon crushed red pepper
2	pounds mussels, scrubbed and debearded
2	dozen littleneck clams, scrubbed
$2/3$	cup loosely packed fresh parsley leaves, coarsely chopped
	lemon and/or lime wedges
	French bread slices

1. Prepare grill for covered direct grilling over medium-high heat.
2. Place butter and oil in large disposable foil roasting pan (about 16" by $12^1/2$"). Place pan on grill over medium-high heat and heat until butter has melted. Remove pan from grill. Add garlic, shallot, wine, and crushed red pepper; stir to combine. Add mussels and clams; spread evenly in pan. Cover pan tightly with foil. Return pan to grill; cover grill and cook 8 to 10 minutes, until mussels and clams open, transferring mussels and clams to warm bowl as they open.
3. Discard any mussels or clams that have not opened. Sprinkle with parsley and serve with any broth in pan, lemon and lime wedges, and French bread.

Each serving: About 286 calories, 18g protein, 8g carbohydrate, 20g total fat (8g saturated), 74mg cholesterol, 282mg sodium.

When buying clams and mussels, the most important thing to look for is tightly closed shells. To test one with a slightly open shell, tap it gently. If it is still alive, the shell will snap shut; if not, it should be discarded. Discard any mussels that have cracked shells, that feel heavy (they may be full of sand), or that feel light and loose when shaken (they may be dead). If possible, cook mussels the day they are purchased. If not, store them in the coldest part of the refrigerator for up to two days.

Mussels with Capers and White Wine

TOTAL TIME 25 minutes
MAKES 4 servings

This recipe is also terrific with clams (the cooking time will remain the same). Serve it with a big loaf of crusty bread to sop up the luscious broth.

1 tablespoon butter or margarine
1 medium shallot, finely chopped (2 tablespoons)
2 garlic cloves, crushed with garlic press
1/2 cup dry white wine
2 tablespoons drained capers
3 pounds mussels, scrubbed and debearded
1/2 cup loosely packed fresh parsley leaves, chopped

1. In 5- to 6-quart saucepot or Dutch oven, melt butter over medium-high heat. Add shallot and garlic and cook, stirring frequently, 2 minutes. Stir in wine and capers and heat to boiling; boil 2 minutes.

2. Add mussels to saucepot. Reduce heat; cover and simmer 10 minutes, until mussels open, transferring mussels to bowl as they open. Discard any mussels that have not opened.

3. Transfer mussels and broth to bowls; sprinkle with parsley.

Each serving: About 201 calories, 21g protein, 9g carbohydrate, 7g total fat (3g saturated), 55mg cholesterol, 650mg sodium.

Honey-Mustard Salmon with Baby Lettuce Salad

TOTAL TIME 20 minutes

MAKES 4 servings

Honey-Mustard Salmon

2	tablespoons Dijon mustard
1	tablespoon honey
1/4	teaspoon salt
1/4	teaspoon freshly ground black pepper
4	salmon fillets (6 ounces each), with skin

Baby Lettuce Salad

1	Gala or Red Delicious apple, not peeled
2	tablespoons seasoned rice vinegar
1	tablespoon extra-virgin olive oil
1/8	teaspoon salt
1/8	teaspoon freshly ground black pepper
1	bag (5 ounces) baby salad greens (about 4 cups)
	lemon wedges

To prevent the salmon from sticking to the broiler rack, spray the skin side of the fillets with a light coating of nonstick cooking oil before placing them on the rack.

1. Prepare salmon: Preheat broiler. In small bowl, with fork, mix mustard, honey, salt, and pepper until blended.

2. Place salmon, skin side down, on rack in broiling pan. Spoon mustard glaze over fillets. Place pan in broiler. Broil, without turning, 5 to 7 inches from heat source, until fish flakes easily when tested with fork, about 8 minutes.

3. Meanwhile, prepare salad: Core and cut apple into thin wedges. In large bowl, mix vinegar, oil, salt, and pepper. Add baby greens and apple wedges; toss until evenly coated.

4. Transfer salmon to dinner plates. Serve with salad and lemon.

Each serving: About 385 calories, 33g protein, 14g carbohydrate, 22g total fat (4g saturated), 89mg cholesterol, 585mg sodium.

Sesame Salmon with Bok Choy

TOTAL TIME 30 minutes
MAKES 4 servings

4	salmon fillets (6 ounces each), skin removed
$1/4$	teaspoon salt
$1/8$	teaspoon freshly ground black pepper
3	tablespoons black and/or white sesame seeds
$1/4$	cup reduced-sodium soy sauce
1	garlic clove, crushed with side of chef's knife
1	teaspoon grated, peeled fresh ginger
$1/2$	teaspoon Asian sesame oil
	pinch crushed red pepper
2	bunches bok choy ($1^1/2$ pounds total), cut crosswise into thirds and root ends cut into quarters
1	teaspoon butter (do not substitute margarine)

1. Preheat oven to 375°F. On waxed paper, sprinkle both sides of salmon with salt and pepper. Coat one side of each salmon fillet with sesame seeds, pressing gently to adhere.

2. Heat oven-safe 12-inch skillet (if skillet is not oven-safe, wrap handle of skillet with double layer of foil) over medium-high heat until hot. Add salmon, seed side down, and cook 2 minutes (do not turn). Transfer skillet to oven and bake salmon just until opaque in center, 10 to 12 minutes.

3. Meanwhile, in 5- to 6-quart saucepot, combine soy sauce, garlic, ginger, sesame oil, and crushed red pepper. Add bok choy to soy-sauce mixture; with tongs, toss until evenly coated. Cover and heat to boiling over high heat. Reduce heat to medium and cook, covered, 8 minutes, stirring occasionally. Remove cover and cook until bok choy is tender-crisp, about 3 minutes longer.

4. Remove saucepot from heat. With tongs, transfer bok choy to dinner plates; discard garlic. Whisk butter into soy-sauce mixture until blended. Place salmon, seed side up, on plates with bok choy and drizzle with soy-sauce mixture.

Each serving: About 330 calories, 39g protein, 7g carbohydrate, 16g total fat (3g saturated), 96mg cholesterol, 870mg sodium.

One of the most common vegetables in Asian cooking, bok choy is a member of the Chinese cabbage family. Prized for its mild flavor, crunchy texture (when not overcooked), and versatility, bok choy can be stir-fried, sautéed, or braised, as in this recipe. Look for crisp, firm, brightly colored stalks and leaves. If you want to get a little fancy, use an equal amount of baby bok choy and leave them whole. Bok choy can be stored in a zip-tight plastic bag in the refrigerator for up to four days.

Teriyaki Salmon with Gingery Chard

TOTAL TIME 25 minutes

MAKES 4 servings

Preparing greens like Swiss chard is easy; just take care because the large crinkly leaves can trap quite a lot of dirt and sand. The best way to wash them is to fill a very large bowl or clean pot with cold water, immerse the chard leaves, and swish them around a few times, then remove them, allowing the grit to settle on the bottom. If necessary, repeat the process until the leaves are completely clean.

1½   pounds red, yellow, and/or orange Swiss chard
  3   tablespoons teriyaki sauce
  2   tablespoons thinly sliced green onion
  2   tablespoons coarsely chopped fresh cilantro leaves
  4   salmon fillets, 1 inch thick (6 ounces each), with skin
  1   tablespoon olive oil or canola oil
  2   garlic cloves, crushed with side of chef's knife
  1   teaspoon grated, peeled fresh ginger
 ¼   teaspoon salt
 ⅛   teaspoon freshly ground black pepper

1. Rinse chard; drain but do not spin dry. Thinly slice chard stems; cut leaves into 1-inch-wide pieces. Set aside.

2. In cup, combine teriyaki sauce, green onion, and cilantro; set aside.

3. Grease ridged grill pan; heat over medium-high heat until very hot but not smoking. Add salmon, skin side down; cook 5 minutes. Turn and cook until just opaque throughout, 3 to 4 minutes longer.

4. Meanwhile, in nonstick 12-inch skillet, heat oil over medium heat until hot. Add garlic and cook, stirring constantly, until golden, about 1 minute. Add chard in batches, then add ginger, salt, and pepper and cook, stirring frequently (stir-frying), until chard is tender, about 5 minutes.

5. To serve, transfer salmon and chard to 4 dinner plates. Drizzle salmon with teriyaki mixture.

Each serving: About 320 calories, 38g protein, 9g carbohydrate, 15g total fat (2g saturated), 96mg cholesterol, 1,055mg sodium.

Honey-Lime Salmon

TOTAL TIME 20 minutes
MAKES 4 servings

3	tablespoons honey
1	teaspoon ground cumin
1	teaspoon ground coriander
1	teaspoon very hot water
3/4	teaspoon freshly grated lime peel
3/4	teaspoon salt
1/4	teaspoon coarsely ground black pepper
4	salmon fillets, 3/4 inch thick (6 ounces each), skin removed
3	tablespoons chopped fresh cilantro leaves lime wedges

1. Prepare grill for direct grilling over medium heat, or preheat grill pan.

2. In cup, stir honey, cumin, coriander, water, lime peel, salt, and pepper until blended. Rub honey mixture over fillets.

3. Place salmon fillets, skin side up, on grill over medium heat and cook 4 minutes. With wide metal spatula, carefully turn salmon and cook until just opaque throughout, 4 to 5 minutes longer.

4. Sprinkle salmon with cilantro and serve with lime wedges.

Each serving: About 342 calories, 32g protein, 11g carbohydrate, 18g total fat (4g saturated), 91mg cholesterol, 487mg sodium.

Want to boost the flavor of your favorite foods? Start with freshly ground spices. Use a mortar and pestle or clean coffee grinder to grind the whole seeds and use just the amount you need. For even more intense flavor, toast the whole spices in a small, dry, heavy skillet over medium heat, stirring continuously, until they release their fragrance. Immediately transfer the spices to a bowl and stir them to stop the cooking.

189

Salmon with Olives and Lemon

TOTAL TIME **30 minutes**
MAKES **4 servings**

Once you try this method for grilling fish, you'll be "hooked." Here salmon fillet is wrapped in a foil bag with vegetables and seasonings then placed on the grill so that it steams in its own juices, which preserves the delicate flavors and textures of all the food within. This is a great dish to experiment with. For instance, use thinly sliced fennel instead of the squashes or try these Mediterranean flavors with red snapper.

1 medium yellow summer squash (6 ounces)
1 medium zucchini (6 ounces)
1 extra-heavy-duty foil cooking bag (17" by 15") or
   2 sheets (30" by 18") heavy-duty foil
2 plum tomatoes, cut into $1/2$-inch pieces
$1/4$ cup Kalamata olives, pitted and coarsely chopped
$1/2$ cup loosely packed fresh parsley leaves, chopped
2 tablespoons extra-virgin olive oil
$3/4$ teaspoon salt
1 teaspoon freshly grated lemon peel
1 salmon fillet (1 pound), skin removed, cut into 4 pieces

1. Prepare grill for covered direct grilling over medium-high heat.
2. Trim ends from squash and zucchini. With vegetable peeler, peel squash and zucchini lengthwise into long thin ribbons. Transfer ribbons to foil cooking bag. (Or place on double thickness of foil on work surface.) Sprinkle tomatoes, olives, parsley, oil, and $1/2$ teaspoon salt over squash and zucchini ribbons.
3. Sprinkle lemon peel and remaining $1/4$ teaspoon salt over salmon. Place salmon on top of squash mixture; seal bag. (Or, if using foil, bring up long sides of foil and fold over salmon several times to seal well. Fold in ends to seal tightly.)
4. Place foil packet on grill over medium-high heat. Cover grill and cook 12 minutes.
5. Before serving, with kitchen shears, cut an X in top of foil packet to let steam escape, then carefully pull back foil to open. After opening packet, check to make sure that salmon is opaque throughout and flakes easily when tested with fork. Return packet to grill if longer cooking is necessary. To serve, slide vegetables and salmon onto 4 dinner plates.

Each serving: About 325 calories, 33g protein, 8g carbohydrate, 18g total fat (3g saturated), 65mg cholesterol, 725mg sodium.

Salmon BLTs
with Lemon-Dill Mayonnaise

TOTAL TIME 25 minutes

MAKES 4 servings

1/3	cup light mayonnaise
2	teaspoons chopped fresh dill
1	teaspoon freshly grated lemon peel
4	salmon fillets, 1 inch thick (6 ounces each), with skin
1/4	teaspoon salt
1/8	teaspoon coarsely ground black pepper
8	center slices (1/2 inch thick) country-style bread
4	romaine lettuce leaves
2	medium tomatoes, cut into thin slices
6	slices fully cooked bacon, each broken in half

This hearty sandwich is prepared with a lemon-dill mayonnaise that goes especially well with salmon. You can also substitute an equal amount of fresh tarragon or snipped chives.

1. Lightly grease grill rack. Prepare grill for covered direct grilling over medium heat.

2. In small bowl, stir mayonnaise, dill, and lemon peel until blended; set aside.

3. Sprinkle skinless side of salmon fillets with salt and pepper. Place salmon, skin side down, on grill over medium heat; cover grill and cook, without turning, until salmon is just opaque throughout, 10 to 12 minutes.

4. Meanwhile, place bread on grill rack with salmon and grill until lightly toasted, about 1 minute on each side. Spread lemon-dill mayonnaise on one side of each toasted bread slice. Place 1 lettuce leaf on each of 4 bread slices, folding lettuce to fit; top with 2 or 3 tomato slices.

5. When salmon is done, slide thin metal spatula between salmon flesh and skin. Lift salmon from skin and transfer to plate; discard skin. Place 1 salmon fillet on each sandwich bottom. Top each fillet with 3 pieces bacon and another bread slice; serve warm.

Each serving: About 570 calories, 44g protein, 41g carbohydrate, 24g total fat (5g saturated), 108mg cholesterol, 955mg sodium.

Parsley-Pesto Salmon

TOTAL TIME 25 minutes

MAKES 4 servings

This is an easy way to liven up some salmon steaks and get supper on the table in record time. If you're feeling adventurous, try this dish with basil or cilantro instead of parsley. Serve it with a simple salad of arugula and sliced plum tomatoes, if desired.

1	cup chopped fresh parsley
1/4	cup olive oil
2	tablespoons fresh lemon juice
1/2	teaspoon salt
1/4	teaspoon freshly ground black pepper
4	salmon steaks, 3/4 inch thick (4 ounces each), skin removed

1. Preheat oven to 400°F. In blender or food processor with knife blade attached, puree parsley, oil, lemon juice, salt, and pepper until smooth. Coat salmon steaks with parsley mixture.

2. Heat oven-safe 10-inch skillet (if skillet is not oven-safe, wrap handle of skillet with double layer of foil) over high heat until hot. Add salmon and cook until lightly browned on both sides, about 2 minutes.

3. Place skillet in oven. Roast salmon until just opaque throughout, 8 to 10 minutes.

Each serving: About 334 calories, 23g protein, 2g carbohydrate, 21g total fat (4g saturated), 67mg cholesterol, 366mg sodium.

Succotash with Grilled Salmon

TOTAL TIME 30 minutes

MAKES 4 servings

1	package (10 ounces) frozen baby lima beans or 2 cups frozen shelled edamame
2	slices bacon, cut crosswise into $1/4$-inch pieces
1	medium onion, chopped
1	stalk celery, finely chopped
2	cups corn kernels cut from cobs (4 ears)
$1/4$	cup chicken broth or water
1	teaspoon salt
$1/4$	teaspoon freshly ground black pepper
4	salmon steaks, $3/4$ inch thick (6 ounces each), skin removed
2	tablespoons chopped fresh chives or sliced green onions

1. Lightly grease grill rack. Prepare grill for covered direct grilling over medium heat.

2. Meanwhile, rinse beans under hot running water until they begin to thaw; drain. In 12-inch skillet, cook bacon over medium heat until browned. With slotted spoon, transfer bacon to paper towels to drain.

3. Add onion and celery to bacon drippings in skillet. Cook over medium-high heat, stirring frequently, until vegetables are tender and golden, about 5 minutes. Stir in lima beans, corn, broth, $1/2$ teaspoon salt, and $1/8$ teaspoon pepper. Reduce heat to low; cover and simmer until heated through, about 2 minutes. Remove from skillet; keep warm.

4. Sprinkle both sides of salmon with remaining $1/2$ teaspoon salt and $1/8$ teaspoon pepper. Place salmon on grill over medium heat; cover grill and cook, turning once, until just opaque throughout, 8 to 9 minutes. Transfer salmon to platter.

5. Just before serving, stir chives and bacon into succotash. Serve succotash with salmon.

Each serving: About 525 calories, 44g protein, 36g carbohydrate, 23g total fat (6g saturated), 106mg cholesterol, 915mg sodium.

Succotash, derived from the Native American word for boiled corn, is most often a combo of lima beans and corn cooked with bacon or butter. If you have the time and access to a farmers' market, buy a pound of fresh lima or cranberry beans. Shell the beans and cook them in boiling water just until tender. Then proceed as directed in Step 3.

Glazed Salmon
with Watermelon Salsa

TOTAL TIME 30 minutes
MAKES 4 servings

This refreshing fruit-based salsa is the perfect complement for the Asian flavors of the glaze on the salmon. It would work equally well with many other spicy dishes. So put it near the top of your list of accompaniments. If watermelon is out of season, try preparing the salsa with fresh orange segments (avoid canned mandarins) or pineapple chunks (drained canned is okay).

1 lime
4 cups (1 1/2-inch cubes) seedless watermelon (from 2 1/2-pound piece)
1/4 cup loosely packed fresh mint leaves, chopped
2 tablespoons chopped green onions
1 small jalapeño chile, seeded and finely chopped (1 tablespoon)
1/4 cup hoisin sauce
1/2 teaspoon Chinese five-spice powder
4 salmon steaks, 1 inch thick (6 ounces each), skin removed

1. Prepare grill for covered direct grilling over medium heat.

2. Meanwhile, prepare salsa: From lime, grate 1 teaspoon peel and squeeze 1 tablespoon juice. In serving bowl, toss lime peel and juice with watermelon, mint, green onions, and jalapeño. Makes about 3 2/3 cups.

3. In cup, with fork, stir hoisin sauce and five-spice powder until blended.

4. Place salmon steaks on grill over medium heat and brush with half of hoisin mixture. Cover grill and grill salmon 3 minutes. Turn salmon and brush with remaining hoisin mixture; cover and grill 3 minutes. Turn salmon again and grill until just opaque throughout, about 3 minutes longer. Serve salmon with watermelon salsa.

Each serving: About 345 calories, 30g protein, 18g carbohydrate, 17g total fat (3g saturated), 81mg cholesterol, 260mg sodium.

Halibut in Thai Curry Sauce

TOTAL TIME 30 minutes
MAKES 4 servings

- 1 cup basmati or jasmine rice
- 1 can (13$\frac{1}{2}$ to 14 ounces) light coconut milk (not cream of coconut)
- 1 teaspoon grated, peeled fresh ginger
- 1 teaspoon brown sugar
- $\frac{1}{2}$ teaspoon Thai red or green curry paste or curry powder
- 1 garlic clove, finely chopped
- 4 pieces halibut fillet (6 ounces each), skin removed
- 2 green onions, chopped
- $\frac{1}{4}$ cup firmly packed fresh cilantro leaves, chopped
- 1 lime, cut into wedges

1. Prepare rice as label directs.

2. Meanwhile, in nonstick 12-inch skillet, whisk coconut milk, ginger, brown sugar, curry paste, and garlic until blended; heat to boiling over high heat, stirring. Reduce heat to medium-low and simmer, stirring occasionally, 5 minutes.

3. Add halibut fillets to skillet and cook, turning once, until just opaque throughout, 8 to 10 minutes. Transfer halibut to warm deep platter.

4. Remove skillet from heat. Stir green onions and cilantro into sauce in skillet; pour sauce over halibut. Serve with lime wedges and rice.

Each serving: About 367 calories, 38g protein, 23g carbohydrate, 12g total fat (6g saturated), 54mg cholesterol, 114mg sodium.

Curry paste, a flavoring that is widely used in Southeast Asian cooking, is, like curry powder, a blend of many fresh ingredients that can include lemongrass, *galangal* (an underground root that resembles fresh ginger and has a hot, peppery flavor), garlic, onion, green or red chiles, and cilantro. These blends are classified as green, red, or yellow, based on the ingredients they contain. Look for plastic tubs, jars, or cans of curry paste in Southeast Asian and Indian markets and in some specialty-food stores.

Jerk Halibut Steak
with Sweet-Potato Wedges

TOTAL TIME 30 minutes
MAKES 4 servings

Jerk seasoning, a lively blend of dry spices that originated in Jamaica, is used primarily to flavor meat, most often chicken or pork. For this recipe, however, we use a fresher blend: thyme, allspice, ground red pepper, fresh ginger, and chopped jalapeño to pep up halibut steaks.

2	pounds sweet potatoes (2 large), not peeled
2	green onions, finely chopped
1	jalapeño chile, seeded and chopped
2	tablespoons fresh lime juice
2	tablespoons Worcestershire sauce
1	tablespoon grated, peeled fresh ginger
1	teaspoon dried thyme
1	teaspoon ground allspice
2	tablespoons olive oil
$1/4$	teaspoon plus $1/8$ teaspoon ground red pepper (cayenne)
$1/2$	teaspoon salt
4	halibut steaks, 1 inch thick (6 ounces each)
	lime wedges (optional)

1. Lightly grease grill rack. Prepare grill for direct grilling over medium heat.

2. Cut each sweet potato lengthwise in half. Place potato halves on microwave-safe plate and cook in microwave oven on High, rearranging sweet potatoes halfway through cooking, until almost fork-tender, about 8 minutes.

3. Meanwhile, in medium bowl, combine green onions, jalapeño, lime juice, Worcestershire, ginger, thyme, allspice, 1 tablespoon oil, $1/4$ teaspoon ground red pepper, and $1/4$ teaspoon salt. Add halibut steaks, turning to coat. Let stand 5 minutes.

4. Cut each sweet-potato half into 4 wedges. In another medium bowl, toss sweet potatoes with remaining $1/4$ teaspoon salt, 1 tablespoon oil, and $1/8$ teaspoon ground red pepper until evenly coated.

5. Place halibut and sweet potatoes on grill over medium heat. Spoon half of jerk marinade over halibut; discard remaining marinade. Grill sweet-potato wedges, turning once, until tender and lightly charred, 6 to 7 minutes, transferring them to platter as they are done. Grill halibut steaks, turning once, until just opaque throughout, 8 to 10 minutes. Transfer halibut to platter with sweet potatoes. Serve with lime wedges, if you like.

Each serving: About 410 calories, 38g protein, 42g carbohydrate, 9g total fat (1g saturated), 54mg cholesterol, 390mg sodium.

Asian Flounder Bake

TOTAL TIME 20 minutes
MAKES 4 servings

A flatfish prized for its fine texture and delicate flavor, flounder is often called sole, even though all of the fish so called are actually varieties of flounder. (Only imported Dover sole is true sole.) Flounder can be baked, as in this tasty Asian-inspired recipe, broiled, sautéed, steamed, or poached.

1/4 cup reduced-sodium soy sauce
2 tablespoons dry sherry
1 teaspoon sugar
1 teaspoon grated, peeled fresh ginger
1 teaspoon Asian sesame oil
1 bag (10 ounces) shredded carrots
1 bag (5 to 6 ounces) baby spinach
4 flounder or sole fillets (5 ounces each)
1 green onion, thinly sliced
1 tablespoon sesame seeds, toasted (optional)

1. Preheat oven to 450°F.

2. Meanwhile, in cup, with fork, mix soy sauce, sherry, sugar, ginger, and sesame oil until blended.

3. In 13" by 9" baking pan, spread carrots in even layer. Top with even layer of spinach, then top with flounder fillets. Pour soy-sauce mixture evenly over flounder. Bake just until fish turns opaque throughout, 12 to 14 minutes. To serve, sprinkle with green onion and top with sesame seeds, if you like.

Each serving: About 200 calories, 30g protein, 11g carbohydrate, 3g total fat (1g saturated), 68mg cholesterol, 735mg sodium.

Pasta with Mahimahi, Tomatoes, and Basil

TOTAL TIME 30 minutes

MAKES 4 servings

8	ounces multigrain rotini pasta
2	teaspoons plus 1 tablespoon extra-virgin olive oil
1	pound mahimahi fillets, cut into 1-inch pieces
$1/2$	teaspoon salt
$1/4$	teaspoon freshly ground black pepper
2	garlic cloves, thinly sliced
3	cups grape tomatoes (about $1^1/2$ pints)
$1/4$	cup dry white wine
$1/2$	cup firmly packed small fresh basil leaves

1. In large saucepot, cook pasta as label directs.

2. Meanwhile, in deep nonstick 12-inch skillet, heat 2 teaspoons oil over medium heat until hot. Add mahimahi; sprinkle with $1/4$ teaspoon salt and $1/8$ teaspoon pepper and cook, gently stirring, until just opaque throughout, 3 to 4 minutes. Transfer mahimahi to plate; set aside.

3. In same skillet, heat remaining 1 tablespoon oil over medium heat until hot. Add garlic and cook, stirring constantly, until golden, 1 minute. Add tomatoes; cover and cook, stirring occasionally, until tomatoes burst, 4 to 5 minutes. Stir in wine, half of basil, remaining $1/4$ teaspoon salt, and remaining $1/8$ teaspoon pepper; cook, uncovered, 1 minute.

4. Drain pasta, reserving $1/4$ cup pasta water. Add pasta, reserved pasta water, mahimahi, and remaining basil to tomato mixture in skillet; toss until well combined.

Each serving: About 380 calories, 33g protein, 45g carbohydrate, 8g total fat (1g saturated), 83mg cholesterol, 500mg sodium.

Mahimahi is a moderately fatty warm-water fish with firm, flavorful flesh. It is widely available as steaks and fillets. In this recipe, it takes center stage in a fresh tomato-basil sauce served over pasta. If you prefer, you could serve it with brown rice instead.

201

Nantucket Seafood Packets

TOTAL TIME 25 minutes

MAKES 4 servings

A popular, widely available saltwater fish, scrod is actually young cod. Like cod, it has lean, firm, mild-flavored white flesh that requires seasoning. Since it is flavor-neutral, it is a very versatile fish that every cook should get to know. Here, it is grilled in individual foil packets with mussels, tomatoes, and zesty lime butter.

3	tablespoons butter or margarine, softened
1	teaspoon freshly grated lime peel
3/4	teaspoon salt
1/2	teaspoon ground cumin
1/2	teaspoon ground coriander
1/8	teaspoon ground red pepper (cayenne)
4	scrod fillets (6 ounces each)
12	large mussels, scrubbed and debearded
2	ripe medium tomatoes, cut into 1 1/2-inch pieces
1	cup loosely packed fresh cilantro leaves, chopped

1. Prepare grill for direct grilling over medium heat.

2. In small bowl, stir butter, lime peel, salt, cumin, coriander, and ground red pepper until blended.

3. From roll of heavy-duty foil, cut four 16" by 12" sheets; arrange side by side on work surface. Place 1 scrod fillet on half of each sheet of foil. Dot scrod fillets with butter mixture. Top each fillet with 3 mussels and one-fourth of tomatoes. Bring up long sides of foil and fold over several times to seal well. Fold in ends to seal tightly.

4. Place foil packets on grill over medium heat and cook, without turning, 10 minutes. Before serving, with kitchen shears, cut an X in top of each foil packet to let steam escape, then carefully pull back foil to open. After opening each packet, check to make sure that scrod is opaque throughout and flakes easily when tested with fork and that mussels have opened. Return packets to grill if longer cooking is necessary. Discard any mussels that have not opened. To serve, sprinkle with cilantro.

Each serving: About 285 calories, 39g protein, 6g carbohydrate, 11g total fat (6g saturated), 103mg cholesterol, 826mg sodium.

Chunky Seafood Stew

TOTAL TIME 25 minutes
MAKES 4 servings

1	tablespoon olive oil
1	medium onion, sliced
1	green pepper, sliced
1	red pepper, sliced
2	Yukon Gold or red potatoes (6 ounces each), not peeled
1	lime
1	can (10 3/4 ounces) condensed Manhattan-style clam chowder
3/4	cup water
1	pound cod or scrod fillets, cut into 1-inch pieces
1/2	cup loosely packed fresh parsley leaves, chopped

To quickly prep the peppers, halve lengthwise and remove the stem end, seeds, and membranes by hand or with a sharp paring knife. Then rinse each half under cold water and pat dry.

1. In 12-inch skillet, heat oil over medium heat until hot. Add onion and green and red peppers, cover and cook, stirring occasionally, until soft and lightly browned, 7 to 10 minutes.

2. Meanwhile, microwave potatoes: Cut potatoes into 1/2-inch pieces. Place potatoes in medium microwave-safe bowl and heat in microwave oven on High just until potatoes are fork-tender, about 3 minutes; set aside. Cut lime lengthwise in half. Cut 1 half lengthwise into 4 wedges; set aside.

3. Stir chowder and water into pepper mixture; heat to boiling. Stir in potatoes. Place cod on top of chowder mixture; cover and cook until fish is just opaque throughout, about 3 minutes.

4. Remove skillet from heat. Squeeze juice from lime half over cod and sprinkle with parsley. Serve with lime wedges.

Each serving: About 295 calories, 25g protein, 37g carbohydrate, 6g total fat (1g saturated), 50mg cholesterol, 420mg sodium.

Steamed Scrod Fillets

TOTAL TIME 25 minutes
MAKES 4 servings

3	tablespoons reduced-sodium soy sauce
2	tablespoons seasoned rice vinegar
1	tablespoon finely chopped, peeled fresh ginger
1	garlic clove, crushed with garlic press
1	pound bok choy, coarsely chopped
1 3/4	cups shredded carrots from 10-ounce package
4	scrod fillets (6 ounces each)
3	green onions, sliced

1. In small bowl, with fork, mix soy sauce, vinegar, ginger, and garlic.

2. In 12-inch skillet, toss bok choy and carrots. Fold thin ends of scrod fillets under to create even thickness. Place scrod on top of vegetables. Pour soy-sauce mixture over scrod and sprinkle with green onions; cover and heat to boiling over high heat. Reduce heat to medium; cook until scrod is just opaque throughout, about 10 minutes.

Each serving: About 200 calories, 34g protein, 12g carbohydrate, 2g total fat (0g saturated), 73mg cholesterol, 820mg sodium.

When shopping for fish fillets, boneless lengthwise cuts from the sides of the fish, make sure they have a fresh briny odor (not "fishy"), firm texture, and moist appearance. As soon as you get them home, refrigerate them, tightly wrapped; prepare them within a day. It's still a good idea to check for the small pin bones that may be lurking. Run your fingers gently over the fillets and pull out any bones you find with tweezers.

Tuna and Cannellini Bean Salad

TOTAL TIME 10 minutes

MAKES 5 or 6 servings

For the most flavor, choose olive oil-packed tuna imported from Italy. This tuna tends to be salty, so before you add the amount of salt called for, taste a bean or two. For an attractive presentation, cut the tops from four large ripe tomatoes, hollow out the centers, and fill the shells with the tuna salad. Serve on a bed of mixed greens, arugula, or watercress.

1 large lemon
2 cans (15 to 19 ounces each) white kidney beans (cannellini), rinsed and drained
1 jar (4 ounces) sliced pimientos, drained
3 tablespoons olive oil
6 tablespoons chopped fresh parsley
1/2 teaspoon salt
1/8 teaspoon coarsely ground black pepper
1 large can (12 ounces) tuna in oil, drained and flaked

1. From lemon, finely grate 1 teaspoon peel and squeeze 3 tablespoons juice.

2. In medium serving bowl, combine lemon peel and juice, cannellini beans, pimientos, oil, parsley, salt, and pepper. Add tuna; stir gently to combine.

Each serving: About 295 calories, 21g protein, 26g carbohydrate, 11g total fat (2g saturated), 9mg cholesterol, 590mg sodium.

Thai Snapper

TOTAL TIME 25 minutes

MAKES 4 servings

3	tablespoons fresh lime juice
1	tablespoon Asian fish sauce (nam pla or nuoc nam)
1	tablespoon olive oil
1	teaspoon grated, peeled fresh ginger
1/2	teaspoon sugar
1	small garlic clove, minced
4	red snapper fillets (6 ounces each)
1	large carrot, peeled and cut into 2^1/4" by ^{1}/4" matchstick strips
1	large green onion, thinly sliced
1/4	cup packed fresh cilantro leaves

1. Prepare grill for covered direct grilling over medium heat.

2. Meanwhile, in small bowl, mix lime juice, fish sauce, oil, ginger, sugar, and garlic. From roll of foil, cut four 16" by 12" sheets. Fold each sheet crosswise in half and open up again.

3. To assemble packets, place 1 red snapper fillet, skin side down, on half of one foil sheet. Top with one-fourth each of carrot, green onion, and cilantro leaves. Spoon one-fourth of lime juice mixture over snapper and vegetables. Fold other half of foil over fish; fold and crimp foil edges all around. Repeat to create 4 sealed packets.

4. Place foil packets on grill over medium heat. Cover grill and cook, 6 to 8 minutes, depending on thickness of snapper. Do not turn packets over.

5. Just before serving, with kitchen shears, cut an X in top of each foil packet to let steam escape, then carefully pull back foil to open. After opening each packet, check to make sure that snapper is opaque throughout and flakes easily when tested with fork. Return packets to grill if longer cooking is necessary.

Each serving: About 230 calories, 36g protein, 5g carbohydrate, 6g total fat (1g saturated), 63mg cholesterol, 270mg sodium.

If you don't own a grill or if you live in a cool climate and there's snow on the ground, you can still prepare this delicious dish. Just place the foil packets on a cookie sheet and bake in a preheated 450°F oven for 10 minutes for every inch of thickness of the fish.

Jamaican Jerk Catfish with Grilled Pineapple

TOTAL TIME 25 minutes
MAKES 4 servings

This spicy recipe also works well with sole, flounder, snapper, and bluefish. If you can't find fresh jalapeños, use one from a jar. Be aware that although fresh jalapeños vary in heat intensity, those from jars are always hot.

2 green onions, chopped
1 jalapeño chile, seeded and chopped
2 tablespoons white wine vinegar
2 tablespoons Worcestershire sauce
1 tablespoon minced, peeled fresh ginger
1 tablespoon vegetable oil
1¼ teaspoons dried thyme
1 teaspoon ground allspice
¼ teaspoon salt
4 catfish fillets (5 ounces each)
1 small pineapple, cut lengthwise into 4 wedges or crosswise into ½-inch-thick slices
2 tablespoons brown sugar

1. Prepare grill for direct grilling over medium-high heat.

2. In medium bowl, mix green onions, jalapeño, vinegar, Worcestershire, ginger, oil, thyme, allspice, and salt until combined. Add catfish fillets to bowl, turning to coat; let stand 5 minutes at room temperature.

3. Meanwhile, rub pineapple wedges or slices with brown sugar. Place pineapple and catfish fillets on grill over medium-high heat. Brush half of jerk mixture remaining in bowl on catfish; grill 5 minutes. Turn pineapple and catfish. Brush remaining jerk mixture on fish and grill until fish is just opaque throughout and pineapple is golden brown, 5 to 7 minutes longer.

Each serving: About 350 calories, 23g protein, 35g carbohydrate, 14g total fat (3g saturated), 47mg cholesterol, 280mg sodium.

Mediterranean Swordfish Salad (Pictured on page 8)

TOTAL TIME 20 minutes
MAKES 4 servings

Swordfish, a moderately fat fish with firm, dense flesh, is available fresh from late spring to early fall and frozen year-round. It's one of the most popular fish in the U.S., perhaps because of its meat-like texture, which can accommodate almost any cooking method, including sautéing, grilling, broiling, baking, and poaching.

3	tablespoons olive oil
1	swordfish steak, 1 inch thick (1^1/$_4$ pounds)
^{3}/$_4$	teaspoon salt
^{1}/$_4$	teaspoon freshly ground black pepper
2	tablespoons fresh lemon juice
1^1/$_2$	teaspoons chopped fresh oregano leaves or ^{1}/$_2$ teaspoon dried oregano
1	English (seedless) cucumber (12 ounces), cut into ^{1}/$_2$-inch pieces
1	pint grape or cherry tomatoes, each cut in half
1^1/$_3$	ounces feta cheese, crumbled (^{1}/$_3$ cup)

1. In 10-inch skillet, heat 1 tablespoon oil over medium-high heat until very hot. Pat swordfish dry with paper towels. Add swordfish to skillet. Sprinkle with ^{1}/$_2$ teaspoon salt and pepper and cook, turning once, until swordfish is browned on both sides and just opaque throughout, 10 to 12 minutes.

2. Meanwhile, in large bowl, with fork, mix lemon juice, oregano, and remaining 2 tablespoons oil and ^{1}/$_4$ teaspoon salt.

3. When swordfish is done, with wide metal spatula, transfer to cutting board; trim and discard skin. Cut swordfish into 1-inch cubes. Add swordfish, cucumber, and tomatoes to dressing in bowl; toss gently to coat. To serve, sprinkle with feta.

Each serving: About 315 calories, 32g protein, 8g carbohydrate, 17g total fat (5g saturated), 68mg cholesterol, 720mg sodium.

CHAPTER 4

Pasta

Pasta Puttanesca with Arugula

TOTAL TIME 30 minutes
MAKES 4 servings

Arugula, a salad green with a refreshingly pleasant slightly peppery bite, adds a nice counterpoint to the sweetness of the tomatoes. Fresh arugula is sold in small bunches with the roots still attached or prewashed in cellophane bags. Look for leaves that are bright green and not wilted. Arugula leaves in bunches can hold an amazing amount of grit, so wash thoroughly and pat dry before using.

1	package (16 ounces) gemelli or corkscrews
$1^1/2$	pounds tomatoes (5 medium), cut into $^1/_2$-inch pieces
1	medium shallot, minced ($^1/_4$ cup)
1	garlic clove, crushed with garlic press
2	tablespoons olive oil
2	tablespoons capers, drained and chopped
1	tablespoon red wine vinegar
$^1/_2$	teaspoon freshly grated lemon peel
$^1/_4$	teaspoon crushed red pepper
2	bunches arugula (4 ounces each), trimmed and coarsely chopped
1	cup packed fresh basil leaves, chopped

1. In large saucepot, cook pasta as label directs.

2. Meanwhile, in large serving bowl, toss tomatoes, shallot, garlic, oil, capers, vinegar, lemon peel, and crushed red pepper until well mixed.

3. Drain pasta and add to tomato mixture. Toss until well coated. Just before serving, add arugula and basil and toss gently until greens are slightly wilted.

Each serving: About 540 calories, 18g protein, 97g carbohydrate, 10g total fat (1g saturated), 0mg cholesterol, 310mg sodium.

Bow Ties with Tomatoes, Herbs, and Lemon

TOTAL TIME **30 minutes**

MAKES **4 servings**

2	pounds tomatoes (6 medium), chopped
1/4	cup loosely packed fresh mint leaves, chopped
1/4	cup loosely packed fresh basil leaves, chopped
2	tablespoons olive oil
1	teaspoon freshly grated lemon peel
1	garlic clove, crushed with garlic press
1	teaspoon salt
1/4	teaspoon freshly ground black pepper
1	package (16 ounces) bow ties or ziti

One of the best tools for grating citrus is a handheld grater with fine rasps, which produces tiny bits of peel that will blend more easily into the sauce than chopped peel. Rasp graters are widely available in larger supermarkets.

1. In large serving bowl, stir tomatoes, mint, basil, oil, lemon peel, garlic, salt, and pepper; set aside.

2. Meanwhile, in large saucepot, cook pasta as label directs. Drain. Add hot pasta to tomato mixture in bowl; toss well.

Each serving: About 530 calories, 17g protein, 96g carbohydrate, 9g total fat (1g saturated), 0mg cholesterol, 695mg sodium.

Gazpacho-style Pasta

TOTAL TIME 30 minutes
MAKES 4 servings

Forget the bowls and large spoons and set out the plates and forks for this clever adaptation of the classic cold soup. All the vegetables—cucumber, yellow and red peppers, onion, and tomatoes—are included, but, in this case, pasta provides the base. If you prefer a little less kick, substitute a pinch of crushed red pepper for the jalapeño. Be sure not to overprocess the vegetables.

1 package (16 ounces) small shells or orecchiette
1 English (seedless) cucumber (1 pound), not peeled, cut crosswise into 1-inch-thick pieces
1/2 medium red pepper, cut into 1-inch pieces
1/2 medium yellow pepper, cut into 1-inch pieces
1/2 medium red onion, cut into 1-inch pieces
1 jalapeño chile, seeded and coarsely chopped
1 garlic clove, coarsely chopped
1 1/2 pounds tomatoes (5 medium), cut into 1/2-inch pieces
2 tablespoons olive oil
2 tablespoons sherry or red wine vinegar
1 1/2 teaspoons salt
1 small bunch fresh parsley, tough stems trimmed cucumber slices and cherry tomatoes

1. In large saucepot, cook pasta as label directs.
2. Meanwhile, in food processor with knife blade attached, pulse cucumber pieces, peppers, onion, jalapeño, and garlic just until finely chopped. Do not puree.
3. In large serving bowl, toss vegetable mixture, tomatoes, oil, vinegar, and salt until well mixed. Reserve 4 parsley sprigs; chop remaining parsley.
4. Drain pasta. Add pasta and chopped parsley to vegetable mixture in bowl; toss well to combine. Garnish each serving with cucumber slices, cherry tomatoes, and parsley sprigs.

Each serving: About 555 calories, 18g protein, 100g carbohydrate, 9g total fat (1g saturated), 0mg cholesterol, 1,045mg sodium.

Fettuccine with Fresh Herbs and Tomatoes

TOTAL TIME 30 minutes
MAKES 4 servings

Ricotta salata, a salted and pressed sheep's milk cheese, is available in some supermarkets and in cheese stores. If you can't find it, do not substitute fresh ricotta. Use a crumble of goat cheese or grated Parmigiano or Pecorino Romano instead.

1 package (16 ounces) fettuccine or linguine
1 cup loosely packed fresh basil leaves, chopped
3/4 cup loosely packed fresh mint leaves, chopped
2 tablespoons fresh rosemary leaves, chopped
1 tablespoon fresh sage leaves, chopped
2 large tomatoes (8 ounces each), chopped
2 tablespoons extra-virgin olive oil
3/4 teaspoon salt
1/4 teaspoon freshly ground black pepper
1/2 cup crumbled ricotta salata
    or 1/4 cup freshly grated Parmesan cheese

1. In large saucepot, cook pasta as label directs.

2. Meanwhile, in large serving bowl, toss herbs, tomatoes, oil, salt, and pepper; set aside.

3. Drain pasta, reserving 1/2 cup pasta water. Add pasta and pasta water to herb mixture; toss well. Sprinkle with cheese.

Each serving: About 565 calories, 19g protein, 93g carbohydrate, 13g total fat (4g saturated), 17mg cholesterol, 920mg sodium.

Pasta e Piselli

TOTAL TIME 25 minutes

MAKES 5 servings

8	ounces (2 cups) mixed pasta, such as penne, bow ties, or elbow macaroni
1	package (10 ounces) frozen peas
2	tablespoons olive oil
3	garlic cloves, crushed with side of chef's knife
1	can (14 1/2 ounces) diced tomatoes
2	cans (14 1/2 ounces each) chicken broth
1/2	cup water
1/4	cup loosely packed fresh basil leaves, coarsely chopped freshly grated Parmesan cheese (optional)

1. In large saucepot, cook pasta as label directs. About 2 minutes before pasta is done, add frozen peas to pot. Cook until pasta is done; drain. Return pasta and peas to saucepot.

2. Meanwhile, in nonreactive 4-quart saucepan, heat oil over medium heat. Add garlic; cook, stirring frequently, until golden, about 2 minutes. Add tomatoes with their juice, broth, water, and basil; heat to boiling. Reduce heat; cover and simmer 5 minutes. Discard garlic.

3. Add pasta and peas to tomato sauce; cook, stirring, until heated through. Serve with Parmesan, if you like.

Each serving without Parmesan: About 317 calories, 12g protein, 51g carbohydrate, 8g total fat (1g saturated), 0mg cholesterol, 1,044mg sodium.

To save valuable prep time, this light variation of *pasta e fagiole* (the classic pasta and bean soup) calls for frozen peas to be added to the pasta while it cooks. But if fresh peas are in season, look for smooth, glossy, bright green pods that are free of blemishes. They are best used the day of purchase and should be shelled just before cooking.

Greek Lasagna Toss with Tomatoes, Shrimp, and Feta

TOTAL TIME 30 minutes
MAKES 4 servings

1	package (16 ounces) lasagna noodles
2	teaspoons olive oil
1	medium onion, chopped
1	can (28 ounces) plum tomatoes in juice
$1/4$	teaspoon crushed red pepper
$1/4$	teaspoon dried oregano
1	pound large shrimp, shelled and deveined, with tail part of shell left on, if desired
$1/4$	cup loosely packed fresh parsley leaves, chopped
2	ounces feta cheese, crumbled ($1/2$ cup), plus additional for sprinkling on top

1. In large saucepot, cook lasagna noodles until just tender, about 2 minutes longer than label directs. Drain and return to saucepot.
2. Meanwhile, in nonstick 12-inch skillet, heat oil over medium heat until hot. Add onion and cook until tender and lightly browned, 5 to 7 minutes. Stir in tomatoes with their juice, crushed red pepper, and oregano; heat to boiling over high heat, breaking up tomatoes with side of spoon. Reduce heat to medium and cook until slightly thickened, about 7 minutes. Stir in shrimp and cook until shrimp are opaque throughout, 3 to 4 minutes. Remove skillet from heat; stir in parsley and $1/2$ cup crumbled feta.
3. Add shrimp mixture to pasta in saucepot and toss to coat. Spoon pasta mixture into large serving bowl. Sprinkle additional feta on top.

Each serving: About 630 calories, 37g protein, 98g carbohydrate, 9g total fat (3g saturated), 153mg cholesterol, 590mg sodium.

Lasagna noodles are tossed with a typical Greek medley: tomatoes, oregano, shrimp, parsley, and feta cheese. Feta is made from sheep's or goat's milk that is pressed into square cakes, and stored in a salty brine. The result is a rich, tangy flavor that can liven up a variety of cold and hot dishes. If you prefer your feta a little less salty, rinse it in cold water and pat it dry with a paper towel before using.

Bow Ties with Shrimp and Fennel

TOTAL TIME 30 minutes
MAKES 6 servings

Fennel seeds, which have a distinctive licoricelike flavor, are used to enhance breads and desserts as well as savories like pork sausage. Here, they add spark to a lovely shrimp dish. If you don't have a mortar and pestle, crush the garlic with a garlic press and place the fennel seeds in a sealed plastic bag, then crush them with a rolling pin.

1   package (16 ounces) bow ties
1   bag (16 ounces) frozen raw shelled and deveined extra-large shrimp
1   cup frozen peas
1   small garlic clove
1   teaspoon fennel seeds
$1/2$ teaspoon salt
$1/4$ teaspoon coarsely ground black pepper
4   ripe medium tomatoes, cut into $1/2$-inch pieces
2   tablespoons olive oil
2   ounces feta cheese, crumbled ($1/2$ cup)

1. In large saucepot, cook pasta as label directs. After pasta has cooked 12 minutes, add frozen shrimp and peas to pot and continue cooking until pasta is done and shrimp are opaque throughout, about 3 minutes. Drain. Return pasta and shrimp to saucepot.

2. Meanwhile, in mortar with pestle, crush garlic with fennel seeds, salt, and pepper; transfer mixture to medium bowl. Stir in tomatoes and oil.

3. Add tomato mixture and feta cheese to pasta and shrimp, and toss until well combined.

Each serving: About 465 calories, 29g protein, 66g carbohydrate, 9g total fat (3g saturated), 125mg cholesterol, 520mg sodium.

Orzo with Shrimp and Feta

TOTAL TIME 30 minutes
MAKES 4 servings

1 1/2 cups (10 ounces) orzo (rice-shaped pasta)
1 tablespoon butter or margarine
1 1/4 pounds medium shrimp, shelled and deveined, with tail part of shell left on, if desired
1/2 teaspoon salt
1/8 teaspoon coarsely ground black pepper
3 ripe medium tomatoes, coarsely chopped
4 ounces garlic and herb–flavored feta cheese, crumbled (1 cup)

1. In large saucepot, cook pasta as label directs. Drain.

2. Meanwhile, in nonstick 10-inch skillet, melt butter over medium-high heat. Add shrimp, salt, and pepper and cook, stirring occasionally, until shrimp are opaque throughout, 3 to 5 minutes. Add tomatoes and cook, stirring, 30 seconds. Remove skillet from heat. In warm serving bowl, toss orzo with shrimp mixture and feta cheese.

Each serving: About 500 calories, 37g protein, 60g carbohydrate, 12g total fat (5g saturated), 197mg cholesterol, 895mg sodium.

If you're not familiar with orzo, at first glance you might think you're looking at rice. *Orzo*, which means "barley" in Italian, is a very slender, seed-shaped pasta that strongly resembles large grains of rice. Here, it provides the base for this Greek dish, but it is also good in soups.

Pasta with Ricotta and Grape Tomatoes

TOTAL TIME 30 minutes

MAKES 4 servings

A simple combination of creamy ricotta cheese, basil and tomatoes is the secret to this flavorful, easy-to-prepare pasta. If possible, purchase the freshest basil you can find on the day you intend to use it.

1	package (16 ounces) penne rigate
1	teaspoon olive oil
1	garlic clove, crushed with garlic press
1	pint grape tomatoes, each cut in half
1/4	cup chopped fresh basil
1	container (15 ounces) part-skim ricotta cheese
1/3	cup freshly grated Romano cheese

1. In large saucepot, cook pasta as label directs.

2. Meanwhile, in nonstick 10-inch skillet, heat oil over medium heat. Add garlic and tomatoes; cook, shaking pan, 5 minutes. Remove skillet from heat; stir in basil.

3. Drain pasta, reserving 1/2 cup pasta water. Return pasta to saucepot. Add ricotta, Romano, and reserved pasta water to pasta and toss until well combined. Top with tomato mixture.

Each serving: About 580 calories, 26g protein, 95g carbohydrate, 9g total fat (4g saturated), 33mg cholesterol, 335mg sodium.

Spaghetti with Oil and Garlic Sauce

TOTAL TIME 25 minutes
MAKES 6 servings

This delicious pasta dish uses the simplest of ingredients with delicious results. Feel free to add some chopped pitted Kalamata olives and/or chopped drained sun-dried tomatoes and serve it with freshly grated Parmesan cheese, if you have those items on hand.

1	package (16 ounces) spaghetti or linguine
$1/4$	cup olive oil
1	large garlic clove, finely chopped
$1/8$	teaspoon crushed red pepper (optional)
$3/4$	teaspoon salt
$1/4$	teaspoon coarsely ground black pepper
2	tablespoons chopped fresh parsley

1. In large saucepot, cook pasta as label directs. Drain.

2. Meanwhile, in 1-quart saucepan, heat oil over medium heat. Add garlic and cook until just golden, about 1 minute; add crushed red pepper, if using, and cook 30 seconds longer. Remove saucepan from heat; stir in salt and black pepper. In warm serving bowl, toss pasta with sauce and parsley.

Each serving: About 362 calories, 10g protein, 57g carbohydrate, 10g total fat (1g saturated), 0mg cholesterol, 361mg sodium.

Things to Add to Oil and Garlic Sauce

Spaghetti with Oil and Garlic is just the starting point for many delicious possibilities.

- Add 4 to 6 coarsely chopped anchovy fillets in oil, drained (or 1 to $1^1/2$ teaspoons anchovy paste) and 2 tablespoons capers, drained, to garlic-oil mixture; reduce heat and stir until anchovies break up, about 30 seconds.
- Add $1/2$ cup Gaeta, Kalamata, or green Sicilian olives, pitted and chopped, to cooked garlic and oil mixture; reduce heat and stir until olives are heated through, about 1 minute.
- Add 2 to 3 ounces crumbled firm goat cheese (chèvre) to tossed pasta; toss again.
- Add $1/3$ cup chopped dried tomatoes to pasta with garlic-oil mixture and parsley; toss to mix.
- Substitute 2 to 4 tablespoons chopped fresh basil, oregano, chives, or tarragon for parsley.
- Add 1 bag (10 ounces) prewashed spinach, 1 can garbanzo beans, drained, and $1/2$ cup golden raisins.

Pasta Ribbons
with Chunky Vegetables

TOTAL TIME 25 minutes
MAKES 4 servings

1 package (8 to 9 ounces) oven-ready lasagna noodles
   ($6^1/2$" by $3^1/2$" each)
1 tablespoon olive oil
2 medium yellow summer squashes and/or zucchini
   (10 ounces each), cut into $3/4$-inch-thick pieces
1 package (10 ounces) mushrooms, trimmed and
   cut into halves, or quarters if large
2 cups tomato-basil pasta sauce
$1/4$ cup heavy or whipping cream
1 small piece (2 ounces) Parmesan cheese

Feel free to use fresh lasagna noodles instead of the packaged oven-ready type. Or, you can substitute dried lasagna noodles or 12 ounces dried penne, cooked according to the package directions.

1. In 4-quart saucepan, bring salted water to boiling over high heat. Add lasagna, 1 noodle at a time to avoid sticking, and cook until tender, 7 to 8 minutes.

2. Meanwhile, in nonstick 12-inch skillet, heat oil over medium heat until very hot. Add squashes and mushrooms; cover skillet and cook, stirring occasionally, until vegetables are tender-crisp, 4 to 5 minutes. Add pasta sauce and cream; heat to boiling, stirring frequently.

3. Drain noodles. In warm serving bowl, toss noodles with squash mixture. With vegetable peeler, shave thin strips from Parmesan. Top pasta with Parmesan shavings.

Each serving: About 515 calories, 19g protein, 70g carbohydrate, 18g total fat (7g saturated), 32mg cholesterol, 770mg sodium.

Orecchiette alla Vodka

TOTAL TIME 30 minutes

MAKES 4 servings

We use orecchiette ("little ears" in Italian) in this restaurant favorite, but rotini is another good option. If there are going to be children at the table, it's fine to leave out the vodka—the flavor will still be delicious.

1 package (16 ounces) orecchiette or bow ties
1 cup frozen peas
1 can (14 to 16 ounces) tomatoes in juice, drained
1/2 cup heavy or whipping cream
1/2 cup milk
3 tablespoons vodka (optional)
4 teaspoons tomato paste
1/2 teaspoon salt
1/8 to 1/4 teaspoon crushed red pepper
1/2 cup loosely packed fresh basil leaves, thinly sliced

1. In large saucepot, cook pasta as label directs. About 2 minutes before pasta is done, add frozen peas to pot. Cook until pasta is done; drain. Return pasta and peas to saucepot.

2. Meanwhile, chop tomatoes. In nonstick 2-quart saucepan, heat tomatoes, cream, milk, vodka, if using, tomato paste, salt, and crushed red pepper over medium-low heat just to simmering.

3. Add tomato-cream sauce to pasta in saucepot; toss until well combined. Sprinkle with basil.

Each serving: About 590 calories, 19g protein, 98g carbohydrate, 15g total fat (8g saturated), 45mg cholesterol, 635mg sodium.

Creamy Rigatoni with Spinach

TOTAL TIME 30 minutes
MAKES 6 servings

1	package (16 ounces) rigatoni or ziti
1	package (10 ounces) frozen chopped spinach
1	container (15 ounces) part-skim ricotta cheese
$1/4$	cup freshly grated Parmesan cheese
10	oil-packed dried tomatoes, drained and finely chopped ($1/4$ cup)
$3/4$	teaspoon salt

1. In large saucepot, cook pasta as label directs. After pasta has cooked 5 minutes, add frozen spinach to pot and cook until pasta and spinach are tender, about 10 minutes longer. Drain well, reserving $1/2$ cup pasta water. Return pasta, spinach, and reserved pasta water to saucepot.

2. Add ricotta, Parmesan, tomatoes, and salt to pasta mixture. Toss over medium-low heat until pasta is evenly coated and heated through.

Each serving: About 420 calories, 21g protein, 64g carbohydrate, 9g total fat (5g saturated), 25mg cholesterol, 580mg sodium.

This pasta sauce is prepared with sun-dried tomatoes packed in oil. Be sure to drain them well and save the oil for salad dressing. Store opened jars of oil-packed tomatoes in the refrigerator. They make a great pizza and sandwich topping and are a wonderful seasoning for sauces and stews.

Fusilli with Blue Cheese and Toasted Walnuts

TOTAL TIME 30 minutes

MAKES 4 servings

This rich, elegant pasta dish couldn't be easier to rustle up. Traditionally it is made with Gorgonzola, a moist, creamy Italian cow's milk cheese with a luscious flavor, but feel free to use your favorite blue cheese.

1	package (16 ounces) fusilli or corkscrews
1	package (10 ounces) frozen peas
$2/3$	cup half-and-half or light cream
$1/4$	teaspoon salt
$1/3$	cup water
4	ounces blue cheese, crumbled (1 cup)
$3/4$	cup walnuts, toasted and chopped

1. In large saucepot, cook pasta as label directs. About 2 minutes before pasta is done, add frozen peas to pot. Cook until pasta is done; drain.

2. Meanwhile, in nonreactive 1-quart saucepan, heat half-and-half, salt, and water to simmering over medium heat. Stir in $3/4$ cup crumbled blue cheese; heat through.

3. In large serving bowl, toss pasta mixture with blue-cheese sauce and walnuts. Sprinkle with remaining $1/4$ cup crumbled blue cheese.

Each serving: About 765 calories, 28g protein, 101g carbohydrate, 28g total fat (9g saturated), 34mg cholesterol, 730mg sodium.

Pasta primavera, which means "spring" in Italian, features one of the season's tastiest harbingers: crisp-tender asparagus spears. These can be pencil thin or thick as your thumb. Neither is an indication of flavor or tenderness, but each has its fans. Asparagus is quite perishable, so use it as soon as possible.

Pasta Primavera

TOTAL TIME 20 minutes
MAKES 4 servings

1	pound corkscrews
2	teaspoons extra-virgin olive oil
1	garlic clove, crushed with garlic press
1	pound asparagus, trimmed and cut on diagonal into 2-inch pieces
1¼	cups packaged shredded carrots
1	pint cherry tomatoes, each cut in half
½	cup freshly grated Parmesan cheese, plus additional for serving
½	cup heavy or whipping cream
½	teaspoon salt

1. In large saucepot, cook pasta as label directs. Drain, reserving ½ cup pasta water; return pasta to saucepot.

2. Meanwhile, in nonstick 12-inch skillet, heat oil over medium heat. Add garlic and asparagus and cook, stirring often, 2 minutes. Add carrots; cook until vegetables are tender-crisp, about 4 minutes. Stir in tomatoes; cook 1 minute. Add Parmesan, cream, and salt; heat to boiling. Remove from heat.

4. Add vegetable mixture and reserved pasta water to pasta in pot; toss to combine. Serve with additional Parmesan.

Each serving: About 640 calories, 22g protein, 95g carbohydrate, 19g total fat (10g saturated), 49mg cholesterol, 670mg sodium.

Linguine with Mushrooms and Ham

TOTAL TIME 20 minutes

MAKES 4 servings

1	tablespoon olive oil
1	large onion, finely chopped
1	garlic clove, crushed with garlic press
1	package (8 ounces) sliced white mushrooms
1	package (4 ounces) assorted sliced wild mushrooms (gourmet blend)
1	piece (4 ounces) deli ham, cut into 2" by $1/4$" strips
1	cup chicken broth
$1/4$	cup heavy or whipping cream
$1/2$	teaspoon salt
$1/8$	teaspoon freshly ground black pepper
1	package (16 ounces) linguine or spaghetti
1	package (10 ounces) frozen peas

1. In nonstick 12-inch skillet, heat oil over medium heat until hot. Add onion and cook, covered, until tender and golden, about 5 minutes, stirring occasionally. Add garlic and cook, stirring, 30 seconds.

2. Add mushrooms and cook, stirring occasionally, until tender and golden, 10 minutes. Stir in ham, broth, cream, salt, and pepper; heat to boiling. Cook, stirring, 1 minute.

3. Meanwhile, in large saucepot, cook pasta as label directs. About 2 minutes before pasta is done, add frozen peas to pot. Cook until pasta is done; drain. Return linguine and peas to saucepot. Add mushroom sauce and stir until well combined.

Each serving: About 650 calories, 28g protein, 103g carbohydrate, 14g total fat (5g saturated), 36mg cholesterol, 1,160mg sodium.

Nowadays time-challenged cooks can purchase a wide variety of packaged presliced fruits and vegetables at the supermarket. It's an excellent tradeoff if you're sprinting to get dinner on the table. For this rich sauce, a wild mushroom blend is the star attraction, so there is no cleaning, trimming, or slicing needed. If it's not available, use all white mushrooms. Make sure that the mushrooms you purchase are not wrinkled or discolored.

231

Pesto Ravioli and Peas

TOTAL TIME 25 minutes
MAKES 4 servings

1	package (16 ounces) refrigerated cheese ravioli
1	package (10 ounces) frozen peas
2	medium tomatoes, cut into $1/4$-inch pieces
1	cup loosely packed fresh basil leaves, chopped
$1/8$	teaspoon salt
$1/8$	teaspoon coarsely ground black pepper
$1/4$	cup basil pesto, store-bought or homemade

1. In large saucepot, cook ravioli as label directs. After ravioli has cooked 6 minutes, add frozen peas to pot and cook until ravioli is done; drain.

2. Meanwhile, in small bowl, combine tomatoes, basil, salt, and pepper; set aside.

3. Transfer ravioli and peas to large serving bowl. Add pesto and toss to combine. Top with tomato mixture.

Each serving: About 510 calories, 23g protein, 55g carbohydrate, 24g total fat (9g saturated), 43mg cholesterol, 705mg sodium.

With store-bought pesto and a no-cook tomato sauce, you can have dinner on the table in less than twenty-five minutes! Feel free to choose ravioli with a filling other than cheese, such as chicken, meat, or vegetables.

Pasta with Sun-Dried Tomato Pesto and Tuna

TOTAL TIME 30 minutes
MAKES 4 servings

This pasta sauce is a simple blend of sundried tomato pesto, lemon and capers. Capers, the flower buds of a bush native to the Mediterranean and parts of Asia, are used to flavor a wide variety of sauces and condiments and also to garnish meat, egg, and vegetable dishes. They usually come packed in brine but are also available packed in salt. In either case, they should be drained (rinse salted ones first), and gently patted dry with a paper towel before using.

1 package (16 ounces) corkscrews or bow ties
1 bag (12 ounces) broccoli florets
1 lemon
1 can (12 ounces) tuna in water, drained
1 container (7 ounces) refrigerated sun-dried tomato pesto
2 tablespoons capers, drained and coarsely chopped

1. In large saucepot, cook pasta as label directs. About 2 minutes before pasta is done, add broccoli to pot. Cook until pasta is done. Drain pasta and broccoli, reserving $1/2$ cup pasta water. Return pasta and broccoli to saucepot; keep warm.

2. Meanwhile, from lemon, grate 1 teaspoon peel and squeeze 2 tablespoons juice.

3. Add reserved pasta water, tuna, pesto, capers, and lemon peel and juice to pasta and broccoli in pot; toss until well combined.

Each serving: About 755 calories, 37g protein, 95g carbohydrate, 25g total fat (4g saturated), 30mg cholesterol, 1,015mg sodium.

Bow Ties with Salmon and Peas

TOTAL TIME 30 minutes

MAKES 6 servings

1	package (16 ounces) bow ties or corkscrews
1	package (10 ounces) frozen peas
2	lemons
2	tablespoons butter or margarine
2	large shallots, thinly sliced (about $1/2$ cup)
1	pound salmon fillet, skin removed, cut into 1-inch pieces
1	teaspoon salt
$1/2$	teaspoon freshly ground black pepper
$1/2$	cup loosely packed fresh dill, chopped

A great choice for company, this pasta with a lemony herb sauce is equally tasty with a blend of Italian parsley and chives.

1. In large saucepot, cook pasta as label directs. About 2 minutes before pasta is done, add frozen peas to pot. Cook until pasta is done; drain, reserving $1/3$ cup pasta water. Return pasta and peas to saucepot.

2. Meanwhile, from lemons, grate 2 teaspoons peel and squeeze 3 tablespoons juice; set aside.

3. In nonstick 12-inch skillet, melt butter over medium heat. Add shallots and cook, stirring occasionally, until tender-crisp, about 2 minutes. Add salmon, lemon peel, salt, and pepper, and cook, gently stirring occasionally, until salmon is opaque throughout, about 5 minutes.

4. Add reserved pasta water to salmon mixture, stirring gently to combine. Add salmon mixture, dill, and lemon juice to pasta in pot; toss gently to combine.

Each serving: About 492 calories, 29g protein, 68g carbohydrate, 12g total fat (4g saturated), 57mg cholesterol, 680mg sodium.

Fusilli with Garbanzo Beans and Spinach

TOTAL TIME 30 minutes

MAKES 6 servings

This lively pasta sauce gets its punch from balsamic vinegar. Premium balsamic is known for its syrupy consistency and sweet, tangy flavor, the result of long aging in wooden barrels. Regular balsamic is not aged and often contains caramel color. Either is fine for this recipe, but if you have premium balsamic on hand, use it.

1	pound fusilli or corkscrews
2	tablespoons olive oil
1	medium onion, chopped
2	garlic cloves, crushed with garlic press
$1/2$	teaspoon dried oregano
1	can (29 ounces) garbanzo beans, rinsed and drained
3	tablespoons balsamic vinegar
$1^{1}/4$	teaspoons salt
$1/4$	teaspoon coarsely ground pepper
2	bags (6 ounces each) baby spinach

1. In large saucepot, cook pasta as label directs. Drain, reserving $1/3$ cup pasta water; return pasta to saucepot.

2. Meanwhile, in 12-inch skillet, heat oil over medium-high heat. Add onion; cook, covered, 5 minutes, stirring often. Stir in garlic and oregano and cook 30 seconds. Stir in beans, vinegar, salt, and pepper; cook, stirring often, 5 minutes.

3. Add spinach, bean mixture, and reserved pasta water to pasta in saucepot; toss gently to combine.

Each serving: About 500 calories, 20g protein, 85g carbohydrate, 8g total fat (1g saturated), 0mg cholesterol, 980mg sodium.

Poblano Rigatoni

TOTAL TIME 30 minutes
MAKES 4 servings

This south-of-the-border pasta toss is only mildly spicy, because poblanos, the peppers that are used for *chiles rellenos* (Mexican stuffed peppers), are among the mildest of chiles. If you can't find fresh poblanos, Anaheims or green bell peppers are good substitutes.

1	package (16 ounces) rigatoni
1	tablespoon olive oil
3	poblano chiles (8 ounces) or 2 large green peppers, cut into $1/2$-inch-wide strips
1	small onion, cut into $1/2$-inch-thick slices
2	small zucchini (6 ounces each), cut into $1/2$-inch-thick slices
2	garlic cloves, crushed with garlic press
$1/2$	teaspoon dried oregano
1	teaspoon salt
1	pint grape or cherry tomatoes, each cut in half
4	ounces Monterey Jack cheese, cut into $1/2$-inch pieces

1. In large saucepot, cook pasta as label directs. Drain.

2. Meanwhile, in nonstick 12-inch skillet, heat oil over medium heat. Add poblanos and onion; cook until lightly charred and tender-crisp, about 7 minutes. Add zucchini; cover and cook 3 minutes. Add garlic, oregano, and salt; cook 30 seconds. Stir in tomatoes; cover and cook until slightly softened.

3. In warm serving bowl, toss pasta with vegetables and cheese.

Each serving: About 635 calories, 25g protein, 100g carbohydrate, 15g total fat (7g saturated), 30mg cholesterol, 925mg sodium.

Pad Thai

TOTAL TIME 25 minutes
Makes 4 servings

1 package (7 to 8 ounces) flat rice stick noodles
    or 8 ounces angel hair pasta
8 ounces medium shrimp, shelled and deveined
1/4 cup fresh lime juice
1/4 cup Asian fish sauce (nam pla or nuoc nam)
2 tablespoons sugar
1 tablespoon vegetable oil
2 garlic cloves, finely chopped
1/4 teaspoon crushed red pepper
3 large eggs, lightly beaten
6 ounces bean sprouts (2 cups), rinsed and drained
1/3 cup unsalted roasted peanuts, coarsely chopped
3 green onions, thinly sliced
1/2 cup loosely packed fresh cilantro leaves
    lime wedges

Pad thai—a tasty mix of noodles, shrimp, peanuts, and eggs—is surprisingly easy to make at home. The trick is to line up all the ingredients before you begin cooking. Unlike Italian dried pasta, rice stick noodles are soaked before they are cooked. Once soaked, however, they require very little heat and so are added to the shrimp mixture near the end of the cooking.

1. In large bowl, soak noodles in enough hot tap water to cover for 20 minutes. Or, break angel hair pasta in half; cook as label directs, and rinse with cold running water.

2. Meanwhile, cut each shrimp horizontally in half. In small bowl, combine lime juice, fish sauce, and sugar. Assemble all remaining ingredients and place next to stove.

3. Drain rice noodles. With kitchen shears, cut into 4-inch lengths.

4. In a nonstick wok or 12-inch skillet, heat oil over medium heat until hot but not smoking. Add shrimp, garlic, and crushed red pepper; cook, stirring, 1 minute. Add eggs and cook, stirring, until just set, about 20 seconds. Add drained noodles and cook, stirring, 2 minutes. Add fish-sauce mixture, half of bean sprouts, half of peanuts, and half of green onions; cook, stirring, 1 minute.

5. Transfer pad thai to warm platter or serving bowl. Top with remaining bean sprouts, peanuts, and green onions and the cilantro. Serve with lime wedges.

Each serving: About 495 calories, 25g protein, 65g carbohydrate, 17g total fat (3g saturated), 235mg cholesterol, 827mg sodium.

Pasta Niçoise

TOTAL TIME 25 minutes
MAKES 6 servings

Want to please the salad devotees as well as the pasta lovers in your family? Try this warm version of *salade niçoise*— the classic French composed salad that features tuna, toma- toes, and green beans—served over pasta. The anchovies blend smoothly into the dressing—giving the dish its robust flavor.

1 package (16 ounces) cavatappi or radiatore
1 pound red potatoes, cut into $3/4$-inch pieces
1 pound green beans, trimmed and cut crosswise in half
2 lemons
$3/4$ cup chicken broth
$1/4$ cup olive oil
2 teaspoons Dijon mustard
$1/2$ teaspoon freshly ground black pepper
2 anchovies, finely chopped
1 garlic clove, crushed with garlic press
1 can (12 ounces) solid white tuna in water, drained
1 cup loosely packed fresh parsley leaves, chopped
$2/3$ cup freshly grated Parmesan cheese

1. In large saucepot, cook pasta as label directs with potatoes. After pasta has cooked 2 minutes, add green beans to the saucepot and cook until pasta and vegetables are tender, about 6 minutes longer. Drain well.

2. Meanwhile, from lemons, grate 1 teaspoon peel and squeeze 3 tablespoons juice.

3. In small bowl, with wire whisk or fork, mix lemon peel, lemon juice, broth, oil, mustard, pepper, anchovies, and garlic.

4. Arrange pasta, potatoes, beans, and tuna on platter; drizzle with dressing. Sprinkle with parsley and Parmesan.

Each serving: About 570 calories, 31g protein, 78g carbohydrate, 15g total fat (4g saturated), 31mg cholesterol, 745mg sodium.

Tortellini in Brodo

TOTAL TIME 25 minutes
MAKES 4 servings

16	ounces cheese or meat tortellini
2	cartons (32 oz. each) reduced-sodium chicken broth
2	carrots, finely chopped
1	teaspoon salt
1/2	cup freshly grated Parmesan cheese
1/4	cup chopped fresh basil

This stick-to-your-ribs soup is perfect for a cold winter's day. If fresh basil isn't available, substitute Italian parsley.

1. In large saucepot, cook tortellini as label directs. Drain.

2. Meanwhile, in medium saucepan, heat broth to boiling over high heat. Add carrots and salt and cook until carrots are tender, about 3 minutes. Add cooked tortellini; reduce heat and simmer 1 minute.

3. Place 2 tablespoons Parmesan and 1 tablespoon basil in each of 4 soup bowls. Add broth, carrots, and tortellini to the bowls and serve with additional Parmesan, if you wish.

Each serving: About 442 calories, 22g protein, 57g carbohydrate, 14g total fat (6g saturated), 56mg cholesterol, 3,471mg sodium.

Thai Noodles with Cilantro and Basil

TOTAL TIME 25 minutes
MAKES 4 servings

Asian fish sauce is made from the liquid of salted fermented anchovies. Highly pungent, a little goes a long way, as well as having an extended shelf life. If you don't have any on hand, substitute reduced-sodium soy sauce.

1   package (7 to 8 ounces) rice stick noodles
1   tablespoon vegetable oil
4   garlic cloves, thinly sliced
     3-inch piece fresh ginger, peeled, cut into thin slivers
1   medium onion, thinly sliced
12   ounces lean (90%) ground beef
1/2 cup chicken broth
3   tablespoons Asian fish sauce (nam pla or nuoc nam)
1   teaspoon sugar
3/4 teaspoon crushed red pepper
1/4 cup chopped fresh cilantro
1/4 cup sliced fresh basil
1   small cucumber, cut lengthwise in half and
       thinly sliced crosswise
1/2 cup bean sprouts, rinsed and drained
1/4 cup unsalted peanuts, chopped
1   lime, cut into wedges

1. In large bowl, soak rice stick noodles in enough hot water to cover for 15 minutes. (Do not soak longer or noodles may become too soft.) Drain.

2. Meanwhile, heat oil in 12-inch skillet over medium heat. Add garlic, ginger, and onion; cook, stirring occasionally, until golden, 8 to 10 minutes. Stir in beef; cook, stirring and breaking up beef with side of spoon, until meat is no longer pink, about 5 minutes. Stir in broth, fish sauce, sugar, and crushed red pepper; simmer, uncovered, until thickened slightly, about 5 minutes.

3. Add drained noodles, cilantro, and basil to beef mixture; cook, stirring, until heated through. Divide noodle mixture among 4 bowls; top each with cucumber, bean sprouts, and peanuts. Serve with lime wedges.

Each serving: About 455 calories, 25g protein, 60g carbohydrate, 14g total fat (3g saturated), 40mg cholesterol, 720mg sodium.

Whole-Wheat Spaghetti with Fontina and Ham

TOTAL TIME 30 minutes
MAKES 4 servings

This cheesy spaghetti is equally delicious with Italian, Danish, or domestic Fontina.

1 package (16 ounces) whole-wheat spaghetti
2 tablespoons olive oil
2 bunches green onions, cut on diagonal into $^{1}/_{2}$-inch pieces
1 garlic clove, crushed with garlic press
$^{1}/_{4}$ teaspoon crushed red pepper
$^{1}/_{2}$ teaspoon salt
1 cup chicken broth
4 ounces Fontina cheese, shredded (1 cup)
4 ounces sliced cooked ham (preferably baked), cut into 2" by $^{1}/_{4}$" strips

1. In large saucepot, cook pasta as label directs. Drain and return to saucepot.

2. Meanwhile, in nonstick 12-inch skillet, heat oil over medium heat until hot. Add green onions and cook, stirring occasionally, until lightly golden, 2 to 3 minutes. Add garlic, crushed red pepper, and salt; cook, stirring, 30 seconds. Stir in broth and heat to boiling. Add broth mixture, cheese, and ham to spaghetti in saucepot; toss until well combined.

Each serving: About 640 calories, 31g protein, 92g carbohydrate, 20g total fat (8g saturated), 48mg cholesterol, 1,290mg sodium.

Spaghetti with Ricotta and Peas

TOTAL TIME 25 minutes

MAKES 4 servings

1	package (16 ounces) thin spaghetti or vermicelli
1	package (10 ounces) frozen peas
4	slices bacon
1	medium onion, finely chopped
1	container (15 ounces) part-skim ricotta cheese
$1/2$	cup freshly grated Pecorino Romano or Parmesan cheese
$1/2$	teaspoon salt
$1/2$	teaspoon coarsely ground black pepper

Cooked crumbled bacon gives this spaghetti sauce its spark. If you want to be more authentic, use a comparable amount of Italian pancetta (see page 248).

1. In large saucepot, cook pasta as label directs. About 2 minutes before pasta is done, add frozen peas to pot. Cook until pasta is done; drain, reserving 1 cup pasta water. Return pasta and peas to saucepot.

2. Meanwhile, in 12-inch skillet, cook bacon over medium heat until browned. With slotted spoon, transfer to paper towels to drain. Discard all but 1 tablespoon bacon drippings from skillet. Add onion and cook until tender and golden, 8 to 10 minutes.

3. Add onion, ricotta, Pecorino, salt, pepper, and reserved pasta water to pasta and peas in saucepot; toss to combine. Crumble in bacon; toss again.

Each serving: About 745 calories, 37g protein, 103g carbohydrate, 20g total fat (10g saturated), 54mg cholesterol, 880mg sodium.

Penne Rigate with Sweet-and-Spicy Picadillo Sauce

TOTAL TIME 25 minutes
MAKES 6 servings

- 1 package (16 ounces) penne rigate, bow ties, or radiatore, preferably whole wheat
- 2 teaspoons olive oil
- 1 small onion, finely chopped
- 2 garlic cloves, crushed with garlic press
- 1/4 teaspoon ground cinnamon
- 1/8 to 1/4 teaspoon ground red pepper (cayenne)
- 12 ounces lean (90%) ground beef
- 1/2 teaspoon salt
- 1 can (14 1/2 ounces) whole tomatoes in puree (if unavailable, use whole tomatoes in juice), preferably reduced sodium
- 1/2 cup dark seedless raisins
- 1/4 cup chopped pimiento-stuffed olives (salad olives), drained

This spicy-sweet spaghetti with meat sauce features pica-dillo: a popular Latin American dish made with ground pork and beef or veal, tomatoes, garlic, onions, raisins, and olives. You might want to double the sauce and serve the leftovers with black beans and rice, as they do in Cuba.

1. In large saucepot, cook pasta as label directs. Drain, reserving 1 cup pasta water. Return pasta to saucepot.

2. Meanwhile, in nonstick 12-inch skillet, heat olive oil over medium heat until hot. Add onion and cook, stirring frequently, until tender, about 5 minutes. Stir in garlic, cinnamon, and ground red pepper; cook 30 seconds. Add ground beef and salt and cook, stirring and breaking up meat with side of spoon, until beef begins to brown, about 5 minutes. Spoon off any excess fat as necessary. Stir in tomatoes with their puree, raisins, and olives, breaking up tomatoes with side of spoon. Cook until sauce thickens slightly, about 5 minutes longer.

3. Add ground-beef mixture and reserved pasta water to pasta in saucepot and toss until well combined. Season with salt to taste.

Each serving: About 452 calories, 22g protein, 67g carbohydrate, 12g total fat (3g saturated), 37mg cholesterol, 175mg sodium (if using reduced-sodium tomatoes).

Radiatore with Arugula, Tomatoes, and Pancetta

TOTAL TIME 30 minutes
MAKES 4 servings

Pancetta is a flavorful Italian bacon with a moist, silky texture. Unlike American bacon, it is not smoked but rather rubbed with a mixture of salt and savory spices. It is sometimes rolled into a tight cylinder before curing for at least 2 months. Pancetta is available at some butcher shops and deli counters as well as presliced and packed in plastic in the prepared meats case at many supermarkets.

1 package (16 ounces) radiatore or corkscrews
4 ounces sliced pancetta or bacon, cut into $1/4$-inch-thick pieces
1 garlic clove, crushed with garlic press
1 container (16 ounces) cherry tomatoes, each cut into quarters
$1/2$ teaspoon salt
$1/4$ teaspoon coarsely ground black pepper
8 ounces arugula, trimmed
$1/4$ cup freshly grated Parmesan cheese shredded Parmesan cheese

1. In large saucepot, cook pasta as label directs. Drain and return to saucepot.

2. Meanwhile, in nonstick 10-inch skillet, cook pancetta over medium heat, stirring occasionally, until lightly browned. (If using bacon, discard all but 1 tablespoon bacon drippings.) Add garlic and cook, stirring, 30 seconds. Add tomatoes, salt, and pepper and cook 1 to 2 minutes longer. Remove skillet from heat; cover and keep warm.

3. Add pancetta mixture, arugula, and grated Parmesan to pasta in saucepot; toss until well combined. Sprinkle with shredded Parmesan.

Each serving: About 560 calories, 22g protein, 93g carbohydrate, 12g total fat (4g saturated), 15mg cholesterol, 680mg sodium.

CHAPTER 5

Vegetarian

Florentine Frittata

TOTAL TIME 20 minutes
MAKES 4 servings

A frittata, which is a thin flat pancake-style omelette in Italy, is a quick, no-fuss dish that can be served with toast for breakfast, with soup for lunch, or with a roasted vegetable and a green salad for dinner. Frittatas are delicious hot or cold, and you can substitute any leftover cooked vegetables for the spinach and tomatoes in this recipe. Cut them into small squares and serve them as an appetizer or atop slices of whole-grain bread for open-faced sandwiches.

- 1 package (10 ounces) frozen chopped spinach, thawed and squeezed dry
- 4 large eggs
- 4 large egg whites
- 2 green onions, thinly sliced
- $1/4$ cup crumbled feta cheese
- 3 ounces shredded part-skim mozzarella cheese ($3/4$ cup)
- $1/4$ teaspoon salt
- 1 tablespoon olive oil
- 1 cup grape or cherry tomatoes

1. Preheat broiler. In large bowl, with fork, mix spinach, eggs, egg whites, green onions, feta, $1/2$ cup mozzarella, and salt until well blended.

2. In nonstick 10-inch skillet with broiler-safe handle (if handle is not broiler-safe, wrap handle of skillet with double layer of foil), heat oil over medium heat. Pour egg mixture into skillet; arrange tomatoes on top, pushing some down. Cover skillet and cook frittata until egg mixture is just set around edge, 5 to 6 minutes.

3. Place skillet in broiler 5 to 6 inches from heat source and broil frittata until just set in center, 4 to 5 minutes. Sprinkle with remaining $1/4$ cup mozzarella; broil until cheese melts, about 1 minute longer.

4. To serve, loosen frittata from skillet. Leave frittata in skillet or slide onto warm platter; cut into wedges.

Each serving: About 230 calories, 18g protein, 6g carbohydrate, 14g total fat (6g saturated), 233mg cholesterol, 570mg sodium.

Capellini Frittata

TOTAL TIME 20 minutes
MAKES 4 servings

This satisfying egg-and-pasta custard is a great way to use leftover spaghetti. Substitute 1 cup left-over spaghetti for the cooked capellini. Serve with a green salad tossed with our Quick Spicy Tomato Dressing (see below) and a chunk of hearty peasant bread.

To prepare dressing: In small bowl or jar, combine 1 can (5^1/$_2$ ounces) spicy-hot vegetable juice, 3 tablespoons red wine vinegar, 1 tablespoon olive oil, 1 garlic clove, crushed with garlic press, ^{1}/$_2$ teaspoon sugar, and ^{1}/$_2$ teaspoon dry mustard. With wire whisk or fork, mix (or cover jar and shake) until blended. Cover and refrigerate. Stir or shake before using.

2	ounces capellini or angel hair pasta, broken into pieces (about ^{1}/$_2$ cup)
2	teaspoons olive oil
1	small onion, thinly sliced
1	small red pepper, chopped
6	large egg whites
2	large eggs
^{1}/$_3$	cup freshly grated Parmesan cheese
^{1}/$_4$	cup skim milk
^{1}/$_2$	teaspoon salt
^{1}/$_4$	teaspoon hot pepper sauce

1. In 2-quart saucepan, cook pasta as label directs. Drain.

2. Meanwhile, preheat oven to 425°F. In nonstick 10-inch skillet with oven-safe handle (if handle is not oven-safe, wrap with double layer of foil), heat oil over medium heat. Add onion and red pepper and cook, stirring frequently, until vegetables are tender, about 7 minutes.

3. In large bowl, with wire whisk or fork, beat egg whites, whole eggs, Parmesan, milk, salt, and hot pepper sauce; stir in drained pasta. Pour egg mixture over onion mixture; cover and cook until set around the edge, about 3 minutes. Remove cover and place in oven. Bake until frittata is set in center, about 6 minutes longer.

4. To serve, invert frittata onto serving plate and cut into wedges.

Each serving: About 190 calories, 15g protein, 15g carbohydrate, 8g total fat (3g saturated), 113mg cholesterol, 545mg sodium.

Mexican Potato Frittata

TOTAL TIME 25 minutes
MAKES 4 servings

1	teaspoon olive oil
12	ounces red potatoes, cut into $1/2$-inch pieces
6	large eggs
1	jar (11 to 12 ounces) medium-hot salsa
$1/2$	teaspoon salt
$1/4$	teaspoon coarsely ground black pepper
$1/4$	cup shredded sharp Cheddar cheese (1 ounce)
1	medium tomato, cut into $1/2$-inch pieces

1. Preheat oven to 425°F. In nonstick 10-inch skillet with oven-safe handle (if handle is not oven-safe, cover with double layer of foil), heat oil over medium heat. Add potatoes and cook, covered, until tender and golden brown, about 10 minutes, stirring occasionally.

2. Meanwhile, in medium bowl, with wire whisk or fork, beat eggs, $1/4$ cup salsa (chopped, if necessary), salt, and pepper. Stir in cheese; set aside. Stir tomato into remaining salsa.

3. Stir egg mixture into potatoes in skillet and cook over medium heat, covered, until egg mixture begins to set around edge, about 3 minutes. Remove cover and place skillet in oven. Bake until frittata is set, 4 to 6 minutes.

4. To serve, transfer frittata from skillet to cutting board. Cut into wedges and top with salsa mixture.

Each serving: About 235 calories, 14g protein, 20g carbohydrate, 11g total fat (4g saturated), 327mg cholesterol, 795mg sodium.

To round out this dish and add a little color to the plate, serve each wedge with a side of fresh guacamole and tortilla chips. Or prepare a jícama slaw with shredded Granny Smith apples and season with ground cumin and a hint of chile powder for a south-of-the border kick.

Potato Pancakes and Carrot-Parsley Salad

TOTAL TIME 25 minutes
MAKES 4 servings

To add a little color to these pancakes, substitute 1 cup shredded unpeeled raw zucchini for an equal amount of hash browns. Be sure to scrub the zucchini first and pat dry with paper towels.

Potato Pancakes

- 1/2 cup vegetable oil
- 1 teaspoon salt
- 1/8 teaspoon freshly ground black pepper
- 2 large eggs
- 1 bag (20 ounces) refrigerated shredded hash brown potatoes (4 cups)
- 2 green onions, thinly sliced

Carrot-Parsley Salad

- 1 package (10 ounces) shredded carrots
- 1 cup packed fresh parsley leaves
- 1 tablespoon fresh lemon juice
- 1 tablespoon extra-virgin olive oil
- 1/4 teaspoon salt

   applesauce and sour cream

1. Preheat oven to 250°F. Line cookie sheet with paper towels.
2. Prepare pancakes: In 12-inch skillet, heat oil over medium-high heat until very hot. In bowl, mix salt, pepper, and eggs. Add potatoes and green onions and stir until well mixed.
3. Drop mixture by scant 1/2 cups into hot oil to make 4 pancakes; flatten each into 4-inch oval. Cook until golden on both sides, 5 to 7 minutes. With slotted spatula, transfer pancakes to cookie sheet; keep warm in oven. Repeat with remaining mixture to make 8 pancakes.
4. While pancakes cook, prepare salad: In bowl, toss carrots, parsley, lemon juice, olive oil, and salt.
5. Serve pancakes with applesauce and sour cream and sides of carrot salad.

Each serving: About 395 calories, 8g protein, 41g carbohydrate, 23g total fat (3g saturated), 106mg cholesterol, 890mg sodium.

Egg and Black-Bean Burritos

TOTAL TIME 15 minutes
MAKES 4 servings

1	can (15 to 19 ounces) black beans, rinsed and drained
1	jar (11 ounces) medium-hot salsa (1^1/$_4$ cups)
6	large eggs
^{1}/$_4$	teaspoon salt
^{1}/$_8$	teaspoon coarsely ground black pepper
4	ounces shredded Monterey Jack cheese (1 cup)
4	burrito-size (10-inch) flour tortillas

If you like your Tex-Mex fare extra spicy, use jalapeño Jack cheese. Pinto beans are also a good substitute for black beans.

1. In small microwave-safe bowl, mix black beans with salsa. In medium bowl, with wire whisk or fork, beat eggs, salt, and pepper until blended.

2. Heat nonstick 10-inch skillet over medium heat until hot. Add egg mixture to skillet. As egg mixture begins to set around edge, stir lightly with heat-safe rubber spatula or wooden spoon, tilting pan to allow uncooked egg mixture to flow toward side of pan. Continue cooking until edges are set to desired doneness, 4 to 6 minutes. Remove skillet from heat; sprinkle cheese evenly over eggs.

3. Meanwhile, in microwave oven, heat black bean mixture on High, stirring once, until heated through, 1 to 2 minutes. Cover and keep warm. Stack tortillas and place between two damp microwave-safe paper towels. In microwave oven, heat tortillas on High until warm, about 1 minute.

4. To assemble burritos, place one-fourth of scrambled eggs down center of each tortilla; top with about one-fourth of black bean mixture. Fold two opposite sides of tortilla over filling, then fold over other sides to form package.

Each serving: About 575 calories, 28g protein, 71g carbohydrate, 21g total fat (9g saturated), 344mg cholesterol, 1,550mg sodium.

Pesto and Mozzarella Pizzas

TOTAL TIME 30 minutes
MAKES 4 pizzas or 4 servings

When you purchase cheese and other dairy products, always check the "sell by" date to make sure you're not buying a product past its prime or just about to be. Store semisoft cheese, like mozzarella and Monterey Jack, tightly wrapped in plastic wrap or foil, in the cheese compartment (or warmest section) of your fridge. To keep it from drying out, rub the cheese with a bit of vegetable oil before wrapping it.

nonstick cooking spray
1 pound refrigerated pizza dough, at room temperature
1/4 cup refrigerated pesto sauce
3 plum tomatoes, seeded and chopped
8 ounces mozzarella cheese, thinly sliced
1/2 teaspoon coarsely ground black pepper

1. Prepare grill for covered direct grilling over medium heat.
2. Meanwhile, spray 2 large cookie sheets with nonstick cooking spray. Divide dough into 4 equal pieces; spray with nonstick cooking spray. With fingertips or rolling pin, press or roll each piece of dough into 1/8-inch-thick round (it's okay if dough is not perfectly round). Transfer 2 rounds to each prepared cookie sheet; cover loosely with plastic wrap. (Bring dough rounds and remaining ingredients to grill for final pizza assembly.)
3. Place dough rounds on grill over medium heat. Cover grill and cook until grill marks appear on underside and dough stiffens (dough may puff slightly), 2 to 3 minutes. With tongs, carefully transfer dough, grill-marked side up, to same cookie sheets.
4. Spread pesto on grilled side of dough rounds; top with tomatoes, mozzarella, and pepper.
5. Return dough rounds, toppings side up, to grill. Cover and cook until bottom of dough stiffens and mozzarella begins to melt, 2 to 3 minutes longer. Transfer pizzas to cutting board; cut into wedges.

Each serving: About 530 calories, 19g protein, 59g carbohydrate, 24g total fat (9g saturated), 47mg cholesterol, 275mg sodium.

Black Bean and Monterey Jack Pizzas

Prepare as directed through Step 3. In Step 4, spread **1 cup pre-pared black bean dip** on grilled side of dough rounds and top with **1 cup shredded Monterey Jack or pepper Jack cheese** (4 ounces). Continue as directed in Step 5 but top with **2 cups thinly sliced iceberg lettuce** and **1/2 cup of your favorite salsa** before cutting into wedges.

Each serving: About 440 calories, 17g protein, 64g carbohydrate, 12g total fat (6g saturated), 25mg cholesterol, 1,080mg sodium.

Arugula and Tomato Pizzas

In cup, mix **1 tablespoon extra-virgin olive oil** and **1 tablespoon balsamic vinegar**. Prepare as directed through Step 3. In Step 4, sprinkle **3 cups loosely packed baby arugula or spinach leaves** on grilled side of dough rounds and top with **6 plum tomatoes** (about 1 pound), thinly sliced, and **2 ounces Parmesan cheese,** thinly shaved with vegetable peeler. Continue as directed in Step 5, but drizzle with balsamic mixture and sprinkle with **1/4 tea-spoon salt** and **1/8 teaspoon coarsely ground black pepper** before cutting into wedges.

Each serving: About 400 calories, 15g protein, 60g carbohydrate, 12g total fat (4g saturated), 11mg cholesterol, 545mg sodium.

Broccoli-Cheese Polenta Pizza

TOTAL TIME 30 minutes
MAKES 4 servings

For this pizza, convenient precooked polenta slices are used as the crust. If you have some fresh basil on hand, chop a couple of tablespoons and stir it into the cheese topping in Step 3.

olive oil nonstick cooking spray
1 log (16 ounces) precooked plain polenta, cut into $1/4$-inch-thick slices
1 bag (12 ounces) broccoli florets
2 tablespoons water
$3/4$ cup part-skim ricotta cheese
$1/4$ cup freshly grated Parmesan cheese
1 teaspoon freshly grated lemon peel
$1/8$ teaspoon freshly ground black pepper
1 large plum tomato (4 ounces), chopped

1. Preheat broiler. Spray 12-inch pizza pan or large cookie sheet with olive oil cooking spray. In center of pizza pan, place 1 slice polenta; arrange remaining slices in 2 concentric circles around first slice, overlapping slightly, to form 10-inch round. Spray polenta generously with cooking spray. Place pan in broiler about 4 inches from heat source and broil until heated through, 5 minutes. Do not turn broiler off.

2. Meanwhile, in microwave-safe medium bowl, combine broccoli and water. Cover with plastic wrap, turning back one section to vent. Heat in microwave oven on High until just tender, about 3 minutes. Drain.

3. In small bowl, stir ricotta, Parmesan, lemon peel, and pepper until blended. Arrange broccoli evenly over polenta. Drop cheese mixture by tablespoons over polenta and broccoli; sprinkle with tomato. Broil until topping is hot, 3 to 5 minutes.

Each serving: About 200 calories, 12g protein, 25g carbohydrate, 6g total fat (3g saturated), 18mg cholesterol, 530mg sodium.

Vegetarian Phyllo Pizza

ACTIVE TIME 15 minutes **TOTAL TIME** 25 minutes
MAKES 4 servings

6	sheets (16" by 12" each) fresh or frozen (thawed) phyllo
2	tablespoons butter or margarine, melted
4	ounces soft, mild goat cheese, such as Montrachet
1	jar (6 ounces) marinated artichoke hearts, drained and cut into pieces
1½	cups grape or cherry tomatoes, each cut in half

1. Preheat oven to 450°F. Place 1 sheet of phyllo on ungreased large cookie sheet; brush with some melted butter. Repeat layering with remaining phyllo and butter, but do *not* brush top layer.

2. Crumble cheese over phyllo; top with artichokes and tomatoes. Bake until golden brown around edges, 12 to 15 minutes.

3. Transfer pizza to large cutting board. With pizza cutter or knife, cut pizza lengthwise in half, then cut each half crosswise into 4 pieces.

Each serving: About 242 calories, 9g protein, 20g carbohydrate, 16g total fat (8g saturated), 28mg cholesterol, 366mg sodium.

To thaw frozen phyllo, it's best to plan ahead. Leave the unwrapped package in the refrigerator for 24 hours. A gradual thaw will produce sheets that are pliable and less likely to stick together or tear.

Ricotta-Spinach Calzone

ACTIVE TIME 10 minutes TOTAL TIME 30 minutes
MAKES 4 servings

Anybody who eats Italian is likely to be familiar with a calzone: a large, triangular pizza-dough turnover stuffed with meat, vegetables, and/or cheese. Refrigerated pizza dough makes calzones a snap to make. For best results, be sure to remove as much moisture as possible from the almost-thawed spinach. Hold the spinach over the sink and squeeze tightly with your hands. Then, place it on a double layer of paper towels, bring up the corners to form a knot, and twist until the liquid is expelled.

1	package (10 ounces) frozen chopped spinach
1	cup part-skim ricotta cheese
1	cup shredded mozzarella cheese from 8-ounce package
1	tablespoon cornstarch
$^1/_2$	teaspoon dried oregano
1	package (10 ounces) refrigerated pizza dough
$^1/_2$	cup marinara sauce

1. Preheat oven to 400°F. Remove frozen spinach from package. In small microwave-safe bowl, heat spinach in microwave oven on High just until spinach is mostly thawed but still cool enough to handle, 2 to 3 minutes. Remove excess water.

2. Meanwhile, in small bowl, stir ricotta, mozzarella, cornstarch, and oregano until blended; set aside.

3. Spray large cookie sheet with nonstick cooking spray. Unroll pizza dough in center of cookie sheet. With fingertips, press dough into 14″ by 10″ rectangle.

4. Spread cheese mixture lengthwise on half of dough, leaving 1-inch border. Spoon marinara sauce over cheese mixture; top with spinach. Fold other half of dough over filling. Pinch edges together to seal. Bake until well browned on top, 20 to 25 minutes. Cut calzone into 4 pieces to serve.

Each serving: About 400 calories, 21g protein, 43g carbohydrate, 15g total fat (5g saturated), 19mg cholesterol, 1,055mg sodium.

Nacho Casserole

ACTIVE TIME 10 minutes   TOTAL TIME 30 minutes
MAKES 6 servings

1	can (10^3/4 ounces) condensed Cheddar cheese soup
1/2	cup lowfat (1%) milk
1	jar (16 ounces) mild or medium-hot salsa
1	bag (7 ounces) baked unsalted tortilla chips
1	can (16 ounces) fat-free refried beans
1	or 2 jalapeño chiles, seeded and thinly sliced
1	cup shredded Cheddar cheese

It's a good idea to always wear gloves when seeding and slicing fresh chiles and do not touch your face, especially your eyes.

Preheat oven to 400°F. In 13" by 9" nonreactive baking dish, stir undiluted soup with milk; spread evenly. Top with half of salsa and half of chips. Carefully spread beans over chips. Top with remaining chips and salsa. Sprinkle with jalapeños and Cheddar. Bake until hot and bubbly, about 20 minutes.

Each serving: About 385 calories, 17g protein, 60g carbohydrate, 12g total fat (5g saturated), 27mg cholesterol, 1,370mg sodium.

If you can't find queso blanco in your supermarket's dairy case, use shredded Monterey Jack or one of the packaged shredded "Mexican" combinations. Sprinkle some cheese on half of each tortilla then fold the other half over. Place the tortillas on a cookie sheet and heat in a 400°F oven until the cheese has melted, 4 to 5 minutes.

Queso Blanco Soft Tacos

TOTAL TIME 20 minutes
MAKES 4 servings

3	green onions, thinly sliced
3	plum tomatoes, cut into $1/2$-inch pieces
1	ripe avocado, pitted, peeled, and cut into $1/2$-inch pieces
$1/4$	small head romaine lettuce, thinly sliced (2 cups)
$1/4$	cup loosely packed fresh cilantro leaves
1	cup mild or medium-hot salsa
1	package (12 ounces) queso blanco (Mexican frying cheese), cut into 12 slices
12	(6-inch) corn tortillas, warmed
1	lime, cut into 4 wedges

1. On platter, arrange green onions, tomatoes, avocado, lettuce, and cilantro. Pour salsa into serving bowl.

2. Heat nonstick 12-inch skillet over medium heat until hot. Add cheese and heat, turning over once, until dark brown in spots, 2 to 3 minutes.

3. Place 1 slice cheese in each tortilla and fold in half. Serve immediately with vegetable platter, salsa, and lime wedges.

Each serving: About 545 calories, 26g protein, 49g carbohydrate, 29g total fat (13g saturated), 60mg cholesterol, 1,300mg sodium.

Couscous Tabbouleh

TOTAL TIME 20 minutes
MAKES 4 servings

3/4	cup water
3/4	cup couscous
3/4	teaspoon salt
1	can (15 to 19 ounces) garbanzo beans, rinsed and drained
4	medium tomatoes (1 1/4 pounds), cut into 1/2-inch pieces
2	Kirby (pickling) cucumbers (4 ounces each), not peeled, cut into 1/2-inch pieces
3/4	cup loosely packed fresh flat-leaf parsley leaves, chopped
1/2	cup loosely packed fresh mint leaves, chopped
1/4	cup fresh lemon juice (from 2 lemons)
2	tablespoons olive oil
1/4	teaspoon coarsely ground black pepper

1. In microwave-safe 3-quart bowl, heat water to boiling in microwave oven on High, 1 1/2 to 2 minutes. Remove bowl from microwave. Stir in couscous and 1/4 teaspoon salt; cover and let stand until liquid has been absorbed, about 5 minutes.
2. Fluff couscous with fork. Stir in beans, tomatoes, cucumbers, parsley, mint, lemon juice, oil, pepper, and remaining 1/2 teaspoon salt. Serve tabbouleh at room temperature or cover and refrigerate up to 6 hours.

Each serving: About 350 calories, 13g protein, 56g carbohydrate, 9g total fat (1g saturated), 0mg cholesterol, 700mg sodium.

Supermarkets now offer cooks a wide variety of fresh herbs, often in quantities that are too abundant to use up before they wilt. But there's an easy way to store any leftover herbs, such as fresh mint or parsley, for future use. Place the herbs in a glass filled with enough cold water to cover 1 inch of the stem ends. Then cover the leaves with a plastic bag and refrigerate up to one week, changing the water every two days. To make chopping easier, be sure your herbs are thoroughly dry.

Vegetarian Rice and Bean Burgers

TOTAL TIME 30 minutes

MAKES 4 servings

For a little extra texture, add a sesame seed coating: Before putting the burgers on the grill, place some sesame seeds on a flat plate, place a burger on top and pat gently to help the seeds adhere. Flip the burger over and coat the other side. Repeat for the remaining burgers.

1	lemon
1	container (6 ounces) plain low-fat yogurt
4	tablespoons well-stirred tahini (sesame-seed paste)
3/4	teaspoon salt
1	package (8.8 ounces) precooked whole-grain brown rice
1	can (15 to 19 ounces) garbanzo beans
1	garlic clove, crushed with garlic press
1/2	teaspoon fennel seeds
	nonstick cooking spray
4	burrito-size spinach or sun-dried-tomato tortillas
2	medium carrots, peeled and shredded
2	plum tomatoes, thinly sliced
1	Kirby (pickling) cucumber, thinly sliced

1. Prepare grill for direct grilling over medium heat.

2. Meanwhile, from lemon, grate 1 1/2 teaspoons peel and squeeze 2 tablespoons juice. In small serving bowl, stir yogurt, 2 tablespoons tahini, lemon juice, and 1/2 teaspoon salt until blended. Set yogurt sauce aside. Makes about 3/4 cup.

3. Heat rice in microwave oven as label directs; set aside.

4. Reserve 1/4 cup liquid from beans. Rinse beans and drain well. In medium bowl, combine beans, lemon peel, garlic, fennel seeds, remaining 1/4 teaspoon salt, remaining 2 tablespoons tahini, and reserved bean liquid. With potato masher, coarsely mash bean mixture until well blended but still lumpy. Add rice and continue to mash just until blended.

5. Shape bean mixture into eight 1-inch-thick burgers. Spray both sides of burgers with nonstick spray. Place burgers on grill over medium heat and grill, turning burgers over once, until well browned on the outside, 10 to 12 minutes.

6. To serve, place 2 burgers in center of each tortilla; top with sauce and vegetables. Fold opposite sides of each tortilla over filling, then fold ends over to form package.

Each serving: About 490 calories, 15g protein, 83g carbohydrate, 11g total fat (2g saturated), 3mg cholesterol, 1,260mg sodium.

Black Bean and Avocado Salad with Cilantro Dressing

TOTAL TIME 30 minutes
MAKES 4 servings

Cilantro Dressing

2	limes
1/4	cup light mayonnaise
1/2	cup packed fresh cilantro leaves
2	tablespoons reduced-fat sour cream
1/2	teaspoon ground cumin
1/4	teaspoon sugar
1/8	teaspoon salt
1/8	teaspoon coarsely ground black pepper

Salad

1	small head romaine lettuce (1 pound), cut into 3/4-inch pieces (8 cups)
2	medium tomatoes, cut into 1/2-inch pieces
2	Kirby cucumbers (4 ounces each), not peeled, each cut lengthwise into quarters, then crosswise into 1/4-inch pieces
1	ripe avocado, pitted, peeled, and cut into 1/2-inch pieces
1	can (15 to 19 ounces) black beans, rinsed and drained

1. Prepare dressing: From limes, grate 1/2 teaspoon peel and squeeze 3 tablespoons juice. In blender, puree lime peel and juice, mayonnaise, cilantro, sour cream, cumin, sugar, salt, and pepper until smooth, occasionally scraping down sides of blender. Cover and refrigerate if not using right away. Makes about 1/2 cup.

2. Prepare salad: In large serving bowl, toss lettuce, tomatoes, cucumbers, avocado, and beans with dressing until well coated.

Each serving: About 230 calories, 9g protein, 34g carbohydrate, 10g total fat (2g saturated), 3mg cholesterol, 520mg sodium.

Not all avocados are created equal. For the richest flavor and creamiest texture, select a Hass avocado (one of the two major available varieties) with dark rough skin that yields slightly to gentle pressure. Avoid any that feel mushy or show mold. After assembling the salad, add the dressing, toss, and serve as soon as possible so that the avocado has no time to discolor.

265

Vegetarian Tortilla Pie

ACTIVE TIME 10 minutes   **TOTAL TIME** 20 minutes
MAKES 4 servings

1   jar (11 to 12 ounces) medium-hot salsa
1   can (8 ounces) no-salt-added tomato sauce
1   can (15 to 16 ounces) no-salt-added black beans,
      rinsed and drained
1   can (15^1/$_4$ ounces) no-salt-added whole-kernel corn,
      drained
^{1}/$_2$ cup packed fresh cilantro leaves
4   (10-inch) low-fat flour tortillas
6   ounces shredded reduced-fat Monterey Jack cheese
      (1^1/$_2$ cups)
      reduced-fat sour cream (optional)

1. Preheat oven to 500°F. Spray 15^1/$_2$" by 10^1/$_2$" jelly-roll pan with nonstick cooking spray.

2. In small bowl, mix salsa and tomato sauce. In medium bowl, mix black beans, corn, and cilantro.

3. Place 1 tortilla in jelly-roll pan. Spread one-third of salsa mixture over tortilla. Top with one-third of bean mixture and one-third of cheese. Repeat layering two more times, ending with last tortilla. Bake pie until cheese melts and filling is hot, 10 to 12 minutes. Serve with sour cream, if you like.

Each serving without sour cream: About 440 calories, 25g protein, 65g carbohydrate, 11g total fat (5g saturated), 30mg cholesterol, 820mg sodium.

Not really a pie per se, this savory main dish more closely resembles a triple-decker quesadilla, with flour tortillas layered with salsa, a black bean/corn mixture, and topped with Monterey Jack cheese. If you want a more authentic flavor, and you have the time, prepare your own salsa, and instead of Monterey Jack, use crumbled queso blanco, if available.

Four Ideas for Black Beans

Low in fat, high in protein, and cholesterol free, black beans are a quick, delicious route to a healthy meal. In all of these recipes, begin by rinsing and draining one or two cans (15 to 19 ounces each) black beans.

1. Black Bean Dip

In food processor, puree **1 can beans, 1 tablespoon fresh lime juice, 1 teaspoon freshly grated lime peel,** and **2 teaspoons chipotle pepper sauce.** Transfer mixture to small bowl and stir in $^1/4$ **cup chopped cilantro leaves** and **2 plum tomatoes,** seeded and chopped. Makes about 2 cups. For a healthier alternative to tortilla chips, try carrot sticks, red pepper strips, or jícama slices.

2. Black Bean Salad

In medium bowl, combine **1 can beans, 1 red pepper,** chopped, **1 can (15$^1/4$ ounces) whole-kernel corn,** drained, $^1/3$ **cup chopped fresh cilantro leaves,** and **2 tablespoons ranch dressing.** Makes about 3$^1/2$ cups. Tastes great alongside grilled chicken or fish.

3. Black Bean Sauté

In nonstick skillet, brown **1 small onion,** chopped, in **1 teaspoon olive oil.** Stir in **1 clove garlic,** crushed with garlic press, and cook 1 minute. Stir in **1 can beans** and heat through. Remove from heat and stir in **1 to 2 tablespoons chopped pickled jalapeño chiles.** Makes about 1$^3/4$ cups. This is a good side dish for pork chops.

4. Black Bean Soup

In 4-quart nonstick saucepan, cook **1 cup fresh salsa** and a **pinch of allspice** over medium heat 3 minutes. Stir in **2 cans beans** and **3 cups low-sodium chicken broth;** heat to boiling over high heat. Reduce heat and simmer 10 minutes. Use immersion blender or potato masher to coarsely mash beans. Makes about 6 cups.

Vegetarian Lentil Stew

TOTAL TIME 30 minutes

MAKES 4 servings

2	teaspoons olive oil
2	teaspoons grated, peeled fresh ginger
2	garlic cloves, crushed with garlic press
2	teaspoons curry powder
1	package (16 ounces) cut-up peeled butternut squash (4 cups), cut into bite-size pieces
1	large apple, not peeled, cut into 1-inch pieces
1	can (19 ounces) ready-to-serve lentil soup
1/4	teaspoon salt
1	cup water
1	bag (10 ounces) prewashed spinach
	lahvash flatbread or pita bread (optional), toasted

The most flavorful part of fresh ginger is just beneath the skin. Use the side of a spoon to remove the skin, following the curves and bumps of the root and leaving as much of the flesh intact as possible.

1. In 4-quart saucepan, heat oil over medium heat until hot. Add ginger, garlic, and curry powder and cook, stirring, 30 seconds. Add squash, apple, soup, salt, and water; cover and heat to boiling over high heat. Reduce heat to medium; cover and cook, stirring occasionally, until squash is just tender, about 5 minutes longer.

2. In batches, gently stir in as many spinach leaves as possible. Reduce heat to low; cover and simmer 5 minutes. Serve with lahvash, if you like.

Each serving: About 190 calories, 9g protein, 34g carbohydrate, 4g total fat (0g saturated), 0mg cholesterol, 650mg sodium.

Sesame Noodles

TOTAL TIME 30 minutes

MAKES 6 servings

Mildly flavored seasoned rice vinegar is made from fermented rice and sweetened (the "seasoning"). It is used widely in Asian cooking, in sauces, and in salad dressings for delicate greens. Here, we use it to balance the sweetness of the o.j. and the peanut butter.

1	package (16 ounces) spaghetti
1	cup fresh orange juice
$^1/_4$	cup seasoned rice vinegar
$^1/_4$	cup soy sauce
$^1/_4$	cup creamy peanut butter
1	tablespoon Asian sesame oil
1	tablespoon grated, peeled fresh ginger
2	teaspoons sugar
$^1/_4$	teaspoon crushed red pepper
1	bag (10 ounces) shredded carrots ($3^1/_2$ cups)
3	Kirby cucumbers (4 ounces each), not peeled, cut into matchstick strips
3	green onions, thinly sliced
2	tablespoons sesame seeds, toasted (optional)

1. In large saucepot, cook pasta as label directs.

2. Meanwhile, in medium bowl, with wire whisk or fork, mix orange juice, vinegar, soy sauce, peanut butter, sesame oil, ginger, sugar, and crushed red pepper until blended.

3. Place carrots in colander; drain pasta over carrots. In large serving bowl, toss pasta mixture, cucumbers, and two-thirds of green onions with sauce in bowl. Sprinkle with remaining green onions and sesame seeds, if you like.

Each serving: About 445 calories, 15g protein, 76g carbohydrate, 9g total fat (2g saturated), 0mg cholesterol, 1,135mg sodium.

Lo Mein with Tofu, Snow Peas, and Carrots

TOTAL TIME 30 minutes
MAKES 4 servings

Tofu is available in blocks of different textures: silken, soft, medium, firm, and extra-firm. Since this dish is stir-fried, we call for extra-firm, which will hold its shape. Tofu usually is packed in water, so you need to drain, rinse, and drain again before using it.

2   packages (3 ounces each) Oriental-flavor ramen noodle soup mix
2   teaspoons vegetable oil
1   package (14 to 15 ounces) extrafirm tofu, patted dry and cut into $1/2$-inch pieces
6   ounces snow peas, strings removed and each cut on diagonal in half (2 cups)
3   green onions, cut into 2-inch pieces
$1^1/2$ cups shredded carrots from 10-ounce package
$1/2$ cup bottled stir-fry sauce
3   ounces fresh bean sprouts (1 cup), rinsed and drained

1. In 4-quart saucepan, cook ramen noodles in *boiling water* (set aside flavor packets) 2 minutes. Drain, reserving $1/4$ cup noodle water.

2. Meanwhile, in nonstick 12-inch skillet, heat oil over medium heat until very hot. Add tofu and cook, stirring occasionally, until lightly browned, 5 to 6 minutes. Add snow peas and green onions to skillet; cook, stirring frequently, until vegetables are tender-crisp, 3 to 5 minutes. Stir in carrots, stir-fry sauce, and contents of 1 flavor packet to taste (depending on salt level of sauce), and cook until carrots are tender, about 2 minutes. (Discard remaining flavor packet or save for another use.)

3. Set aside some bean sprouts for garnish. Add noodles, reserved noodle water, and remaining bean sprouts to skillet; cook, stirring, 1 minute. To serve, sprinkle with bean sprouts.

Each serving: About 375 calories, 18g protein, 47g carbohydrate, 12g total fat (3g saturated), 0mg cholesterol, 1,485mg sodium.

Tofu "Egg" Salad

TOTAL TIME 15 minutes
MAKES 4 servings

1	package (16 ounces) firm tofu, drained
1	celery stalk, finely chopped
1/2	small red pepper, finely chopped
1	green onion, finely chopped
1/4	cup low-fat mayonnaise dressing
1/2	teaspoon salt
1/8	teaspoon turmeric

In medium bowl, with fork, mash tofu until it resembles scrambled eggs. Stir in celery, red pepper, green onion, mayonnaise, salt, and turmeric. Cover and refrigerate up to 1 day if not serving right away.

Each serving: About 195 calories, 18g protein, 10g carbohydrate, 11g total fat (1g saturated), 0mg cholesterol, 455mg sodium.

This mock egg salad takes much less time to prepare than hard-cooked eggs. Use it with shredded lettuce and tomatoes to fill whole-wheat pitas, drop a spoonful on the root end of Belgian endive spears and top with a tuft of alfalfa sprouts to add to an hors d'oeuvre tray, or use it to fill a partially hollowed out tomato for the center of a salad platter.

Thai Coconut Soup

TOTAL TIME 20 minutes
MAKES 4 servings

The classic version of this soup contains sliced chicken. If you like, add 12 ounces thinly sliced chicken breast meat, cut into $1/2$-inch slivers, to the pan instead of the tofu.

- 2 small carrots, each peeled and cut crosswise in half
- $1/2$ medium red pepper
- 1 can (14 ounces) light unsweetened coconut milk (not cream of coconut), well stirred
- 2 garlic cloves, crushed with garlic press
  2-inch piece peeled fresh ginger, cut into 4 slices
- $1/2$ teaspoon ground coriander
- $1/2$ teaspoon ground cumin
- $1/4$ teaspoon ground red pepper (cayenne)
- 12 ounces firm tofu, cut into 1-inch pieces
- 2 cans (14 to $14^1/2$ ounces each) vegetable broth or chicken broth
- 1 tablespoon Asian fish sauce (nam pla or nuoc nam)
- 1 tablespoon fresh lime juice
- 1 cup water
- 2 green onions, sliced
- $1/2$ cup chopped fresh cilantro leaves

1. With vegetable peeler, remove lengthwise strips from carrots and edge of red pepper; set aside.

2. In 5-quart Dutch oven, heat $1/2$ cup coconut milk to boiling over medium heat. Add garlic, ginger, coriander, cumin, and ground red pepper and cook, stirring, 1 minute.

3. Increase heat to medium-high. Stir in tofu, broth, carrot strips, pepper strips, fish sauce, lime juice, water, and remaining coconut milk; heat just to simmering. Discard ginger. Just before serving, stir in green onions and cilantro.

Each serving: About 210 calories, 11g protein, 14g carbohydrate, 17g total fat (6g saturated), 0mg cholesterol, 1,060mg sodium.

Index

Substitutions

Asian fish sauce, 1 tablespoon
Use 2 teaspoons soy sauce and 1 teaspoon anchovy paste.

Baking powder, 1 teaspoon
Use $1/2$ teaspoon cream of tartar and $1/4$ teaspoon baking soda (make fresh for each use).

Buttermilk, 1 cup
Place 1 tablespoon vinegar or lemon juice in cup and stir in enough milk to equal 1 cup; let stand 5 minutes to thicken. Or use 1 cup plain yogurt or sour cream, thinned with $1/4$ cup milk (there will be some leftover).

Cake flour, 1 cup
Place 2 tablespoons cornstarch in cup and add enough all-purpose flour to fill to overflowing; level off top; stir well before using.

Chives
Substitute green onion tops.

Chocolate, unsweetened, melted, 1 ounce
Use 3 tablespoons unsweetened cocoa plus 1 tablespoon salad oil, shortening, butter, or margarine.

Cornstarch (for thickening), 1 tablespoon
Use 2 tablespoons all-purpose flour or 2 tablespoons quick-cooking tapioca.

Light brown sugar, 1 cup
Use 1 cup granulated sugar and 1 tablespoon molasses or use dark brown sugar.

Pancetta
Substitute sliced smoked bacon. Simmer in water for three minutes, then rinse and drain.

Pepper, ground red, $1/8$ teaspoon
Use 4 drops hot pepper sauce.

Pine nuts
Use walnuts or almonds.

Prosciutto
Use ham, preferably Westphalian or a country ham, such as Smithfield.

Shallots
Use red onion.

Tomato sauce, 15-ounce can
Use 6-ounce can tomato paste plus $1^1/2$ cans water.

Yeast, active dry, $1/4$-ounce
package Use 0.6-ounce cake, or use one-third of 2-ounce cake compressed yeast.

Vanilla extract
Use brandy or an appropriately flavored liqueur.

Food Equivalents

Bacon, 16-ounce package, diced, cooked	1^1/$_2$ cups pieces
Beans, dry 1 pound 1 cup	2 cups 2 to 2^1/$_2$ cups cooked
Berries	See individual varieties.
Blackberries, 1 pint	about 2 cups
Blueberries, 1 pint	about 3 cups
Bread crumbs, dried 8-ounce package	2^1/$_4$ cups
Bread crumbs, fresh 1 slice bread	^{1}/$_2$ cup bread crumbs
Butter or margarine ^{1}/$_4$-pound stick 1 pound	^{1}/$_2$ cup or 8 tablespoons 4 sticks or 2 cups
Cabbage, 1 pound coarsely sliced	about 4 to 5 cups
Celery, 1 medium bunch sliced/diced	about 4 cups
Cheddar cheese, 4 ounces	1 cup shredded
Cherries, 1 pound	about 2 cups pitted
Chicken, cooked 2^1/$_2$-pound to 3-pound chicken, diced meat	about 2^1/$_2$ cups
Cocoa, unsweetened, 8-ounce can	2 cups
Coconut, flaked, 3^1/$_2$ ounces	1^1/$_3$ cups
Cookies, crushed chocolate wafers, 20 2^1/$_4$-inch gingersnaps, 15 vanilla wafers, 22	about 1 cup fine crumbs about 1 cup fine crumbs about 1 cup fine crumbs
Cottage cheese, 8 ounces	1 cup
Couscous, 1 cup	about 2^1/$_2$ cups cooked
Crackers, crushed graham, 7 5" by 2^1/$_2$" crackers saltine, 28	about 1 cup fine crumbs about 1 cup fine crumbs
Cranberries, 12-ounce bag	3 cups
Cream, heavy or whipping, 1 cup	about 2 cups whipped cream
Cream cheese 3-ounce package 8-ounce package	6 tablespoons 1 cup
Currants, dried, 5 ounces	about 1 cup
Dates, dry, pitted, 10-ounce container	about 2 cups
Egg whites, large 1 1 cup	about 2 tablespoons 8 to 10 egg whites
Egg yolks, large, 1 cup	12 to 14 egg yolks
Flour, 1 pound all-purpose cake whole-wheat	about 3^1/$_2$ cups about 4 cups about 3^3/$_4$ cups
Gelatin, unflavored, to gel 2 cups liquid	1 envelope
Green or red bell pepper, 1 large	about 1 cup chopped
Hominy grits, 1 cup	about 4^1/$_2$ cups cooked
Honey, liquid, 16 ounces	1^1/$_3$ cups

Food Equivalents

Lemon, 1 medium	3 tablespoons juice; about 1 tablespoon grated zest
Macaroni, elbow, 1 cup	about 2 cups cooked
Milk, evaporated 5-ounce can 12-ounce can	$^2/_3$ cup $1^2/_3$ cups
Molasses, 12 ounces	$1^1/_2$ cups
Mozzarella cheese, 4 ounces	1 cup shredded
Mushrooms, fresh, $^1/_2$ pound	about $2^1/_2$ cups sliced; scant 1 cup sliced and cooked
Oats, 1 cup, old fashioned or quick-cooking	about 2 cups cooked oatmeal
Onion, 1 large	$^3/_4$ to 1 cup chopped
Orange, 1 medium-sized	$^1/_3$ to $^1/_2$ cup juice; 2 tablespoons grated zest
Parmesan cheese, 4 ounces	1 cup grated
Peas, green, fresh in pod, 1 pound shelled	1 cup
Pineapple, 1 large	about 4 cups cubed
Popcorn, $^1/_4$ cup	about 4 cups popped
Potatoes, white, 1 pound	3 medium-sized; about 3 cups sliced; about $2^1/_4$ cups diced; about 2 cups mashed
Raisins, 1 pound	about $2^1/_4$ cups

Raspberries, $^1/_2$ pint	about 1 cup
Rice, 1 cup parboiled	about 4 cups cooked
precooked	about 2 cups cooked
regular long-grain	about 3 cups cooked
brown	about 4 cups cooked
wild	3 to 4 cups cooked
Shortening, vegetable, 1 pound	$2^1/_2$ cups
Sour cream, 8 ounces	1 cup
Spaghetti, 8 ounces	4 cups cooked
Strawberries, 1 pint	about $3^1/_4$ cups whole; $2^1/_4$ cups sliced
Sugar, 1 pound granulated white	$2^1/_4$ to $2^1/_2$ cups
confectioners'	about $3^3/_4$ cups
light brown	about $2^1/_4$ cups packed
dark brown	about $2^1/_4$ cups packed
Sweet potatoes, 1 pound	2 medium-sized; about $2^1/_4$ cups sliced; about $1^1/_2$ cups mashed
Syrup corn, 16 ounces	2 cups
maple, 8 ounces	1 cup
Yeast, active dry, 1 package	about $2^1/_2$ teaspoons

Metric Equivalent Chart

The information on this chart is provided to help cooks outside the U.S. successfully use the recipes in this cookbook. All equivalents are approximate.

Metric Equivalents for Different Types of Ingredients

A standard cup measure of a dry or solid ingredient will vary in weight depending on the type of ingredient. A standard cup of liquid is the same volume for any type of liquid.

Standard Cup	Fine Powder (e.g., flour)	Grain (e.g., rice)	Granular (e.g., sugar)	Liquid Solids (e.g., butter)	Liquid (e.g., milk)
1	140 g	150 g	190 g	200 g	240 ml
3/4	105 g	113 g	143 g	150 g	180 ml
2/3	93 g	100 g	125 g	133 g	160 ml
1/2	70 g	75 g	95 g	100 g	120 ml
1/3	47 g	50 g	63 g	67 g	80 ml
1/4	35 g	38 g	48 g	50 g	60 ml
1/8	18 g	19 g	24 g	25 g	30 ml

Useful Equivalents for Liquid Ingredients by Volume

1/4 tsp	=							1 ml
1/2 tsp	=							2 ml
1 tsp	=							5 ml
3 tsp	=	1 tbls	=			1/2 fl oz	=	15 ml
		2 tbls	=	1/8 cup	=	1 fl oz	=	30 ml
		4 tbls	=	1/4 cup	=	2 fl oz	=	60 ml
		5 1/3 tbls	=	1/3 cup	=	3 fl oz	=	80 ml
		8 tbls	=	1/2 cup	=	4 fl oz	=	120 ml
		10 2/3 tbls	=	2/3 cup	=	5 fl oz	=	160 ml
		12 tbls	=	3/4 cup	=	6 fl oz	=	180 ml
		16 tbls	=	1 cup	=	8 fl oz	=	240 ml
		1 pt	=	2 cups	=	16 fl oz	=	480 ml
		1 qt	=	4 cups	=	32 fl oz	=	960 ml
						33 fl oz	=	1000 ml = 1 l

Useful Equivalents for Dry Ingredients by Weight

(To convert ounces to grams, multiply the number of ounces by 30.)

1 oz	=	1/16 lb	=	30 g
4 oz	=	1/4 lb	=	120 g
8 oz	=	1/2 lb	=	240 g
12 oz	=	3/4 lb	=	360 g
16 oz	=	1 lb	=	480 g

Useful Equivalents for Length

(To convert inches to centimeters, multiply the number of inches by 2.5.)

1 in	=			2.5 cm
6 in	=	1/2 ft	=	15 cm
12 in	=	1 ft	=	30 cm
36 in	=	3 ft	= 1 yd =	90 cm
40 in	=			100 cm = 1 m

Useful Equivalents for Cooking/Oven Temperatures

	Fahrenheit	Celsius	Gas Mark
Freeze Water	32° F	0° C	
Room Temperature	68° F	20° C	
Boil Water	212° F	100° C	
Bake	325° F	160° C	3
	350° F	180° C	4
	375° F	190° C	5
	400° F	200° C	6
	425° F	220° C	7
	450° F	230° C	8
Broil			Grill